ρ

Asian Adolescents in the West

Asian Adolescents in the West

Paul A. Singh Ghuman

University of Wales, Aberystwyth

BPS
BOOKS

THE BRITISH
PSYCHOLOGICAL
SOCIETY

First published in 1999 by BPS Books (The British Psychological Society), St Andrews House, 48 Princess Road East, Leicester LE1 7DR, UK, and 22883 Quicksilver Drive, Stirling, VA 20166, USA.

A catalogue record for this book is available from the British Library.

Library of Congress Cataloging-in-Publication Data on file.

ISBN 1 85433 284 8

Typeset by The Midlands Book Typesetting Company, Loughborough. Printed in Great Britain by Antony Rowe Limited, Reading, Berkshire.

Whilst every effort has been made to ensure the accuracy of the contents of this publication, the publishers and author expressly disclaim responsibility in law for negligence or any other cause of action whatsoever.

Contents

Dedication

To my families in India and the UK with love and appreciation.
And to Taylor-Page, Kerry, Nalini, Michelle,
Shauna (and baby Clara Ffion) and Sean with best love.

Preface

*To judge one culture by the standards of another argues a failure
of imagination and understanding. Every culture has its own
attributes, which must be grasped in and for themselves. In order
to understand a culture, one must employ the same faculties of
sympathetic insight with which we understand one another,
without which there is neither love nor friendship, nor true
human relationships.*
(Berlin, 1990, p. 38)

The history of humankind is replete with examples of migration
from one region of the globe to another. People have always moved
both within and outside national/tribal boundaries to seek work,
to improve their material condition, to escape persecution or for
territorial gain. However, the migration of people to Western Europe,
the US and Australia since the Second World War has been
unprecedented (Cohen, 1991).

Naturally people emigrate with their cultural 'baggage', the essential
elements of which include, amongst a host of other things, religion,
language, myths and metaphors, and social customs and mores. One
of the main features distinguishing humans from the rest of the
animal kingdom is our ability to plan, imagine, communicate and
to develop ontological outlooks and 'world views'. The main
instrument which facilitates these cognitive and affective activities
is language, and one of the major challenges which face the newly-
arrived immigrants is that of learning the language of their host
country through which they may come to understand the prevailing
'mentality', culture and *zeitgeist*.

On migration, the newcomers (unless they are conquerors) usually
try to make changes to their lifestyles so that they can avail themselves
of the opportunities to 'fit in' in their country of adoption. At the
same time, most of them cling to as many of their traditions and
social customs as possible, if only to maintain their personal and
social identities and thus continuity with their past. A few radically

ix

alter their lives in the spirit of the maxim 'When in Rome do as the Romans do', and try to assimilate. This process of 'acculturation' is fraught with difficulties for those immigrants whose language, religion and social traditions are radically different from those of their host society. Further problems of adjustment arise when the receiving society is openly hostile to the newcomers and practises discrimination and exclusion. After the Second World War, immigrants to the UK from the Indian sub-continent (South Asians) and Hong Kong (Chinese) found themselves confronted with most of the problems posed by this predicament.

However, their progeny (the majority of whom are UK-born) face a somewhat different kind of problem. They are growing up (and have been socialized) in *two* distinctive cultural traditions and value systems. Their homes stress the importance of family and kinship (what South Asians call *biraderi*), a traditional role for girls and women and an adherence to the community's religious values and traditions. British society, on the other hand, values individual autonomy, gender equality and a secular outlook. These conflicting values can be a source of psychological conflict and tension in Asian youngsters, for there is an additional handicap for Asian teenagers which their white counterparts do not have to face. There is evidence (Jones, 1993; Modood *et al.*, 1997) of widespread racial prejudice and discrimination against Asians in the employment market, in the allocation of welfare services, and, indeed, in all walks of life. In short, then, UK-born South Asian and Chinese young people have to face additional challenges and problems to those facing their white peers on the journey from childhood through adolescence to adulthood.

The study of adolescence has become a major area of research (see Coleman and Hendry, 1989; Peterson, 1988). Adolescence is a period of rapid growth when physiological and psychological changes can cause serious problems of social adjustment and the development of personal identity. Investigations into adolescence have been conducted from a variety of perspectives, including anthropological, sociological, psychological and ethnographic. The most recent trend, however, is to approach the problem from an interdisciplinary angle (Peterson, 1988; Phinney, 1996; Weinreich, 1996). An understanding of the wider socio-cultural and historical contexts is deemed important, as is the situational context of the young people (Phinney and Goossens, 1996). Additionally, the impetus for interdisciplinary enquiries has come from educational psychologists (Wolfendale *et al.*, 1988) and other professionals who would like to have access to relevant concepts and theories which may enhance their understanding of the issues as well as improve their professional practice.

It is important for those who work, or intend to work, with Asian youths (PGCE undergraduates, teachers, social workers and educational psychologists) in a multicultural British society that they understand the psychological difficulties of Asian youngsters within the broader socio-cultural and historical context. To this end, this book aims to make a distinctive contribution. It builds on the previous work of the author (Ghuman, 1975; 1980a; 1991a,b; 1994; 1996; 1997) and those of the other researchers in the field (Anwar, 1998; Stopes-Roe and Cochrane, 1990; Verma and Ashworth, 1986) and provides an up-to-date picture of the situation of South Asian and Chinese young people currently living in the UK. Nevertheless, the issues raised here should find their echo in other Western European countries, in North America, Australia and elsewhere.

This book is written from a psychological perspective but liberal use is made of studies from the fields of anthropology, education and sociology (for example, Anwar, 1996; Shaw, 1989; Gibson, 1988). The first two chapters are designed to provide a backdrop to the later discussion of the important issues facing second and third generation Asians. These include: inter-ethnic relationships, racial prejudice, gender equality, development of ethnic identity, bilingualism, the practice of home religion and scholastic achievement and adjustment.

Attention is also given to the *positive* aspects of living in two cultures, which are often ignored by the professionals. Bi-culturalism can provide, as it were, 'two windows' on the world. Likewise, the learning of a second language can enhance the understanding of one's first language (Steiner, 1997) and can facilitate all-round intellectual development. Moreover, the tensions and conflicts which might ensue from a clash of cultures can be creatively channelled into art, music and works of literary merit. This can be seen in the recent success of the Punjabi-origin writer, Meera Syal (*Anita and Me*; the film *Bhaji on the Beach*), whose book is based on her childhood bicultural experiences of living in the British Midlands. She projects her thoughts about the Punjabi language on to Anita:

I felt strange to hear Punjabi under the stars. It was an indoor language to me, an almost guilty secret which the Elders would only share away from prying English eyes and ears. On the street, in shops, on buses, in parks, I noticed how the volume would go up when they spoke English, telling us kids not to wander off . . . They switched to Punjabi and the volume became a conspiratorial whisper. 'That woman over there, her hat like a dead dog . . . the bastard is asking too much, let's go'.
(Syal, 1996, p. 203)

Witness also that in classical music there has been a collaboration between Ravi Shankar, an Indian maestro, and Yehudi Menuhin in experimenting with the traditions of the East and West and, likewise in 'pop music', *bhangra* beat (Punjabi rock) has emerged as a new symbol of ethnic identity for South Asian youths in Britain. Even earlier, in the 1960s, the Beatles travelled to India, and were musically influenced by their exposure to Indian culture.

All of these issues will be discussed extensively in this book in relation to the findings of previous research in the field. I have liberally used the comments of young people to give the reader something of the flavour and depth of feelings about the issues which concern them. The literature on South Asian people in the UK is plentiful and is growing, whereas studies of Chinese people in the UK are scarce. Therefore, in the case of the Chinese, I have had to rely on research published mainly from an educational perspective (Wong, Y-F. L., 1992; Wong, L. M., 1989).

Finally, a word about the terminology which is currently used to describe immigrants from the East and which varies from country to country. In Britain, people from the Indian sub-continent are usually referred to as *Asians* and those from Hong Kong and mainland China as *Chinese*. In North America, the term *Asians* is used for people from Southeast Asia (for example, China, Hong Kong, Japan, Korea and Vietnam); for people from India (and possibly from Pakistan and Bangladesh as well because their number is very small) the usual description is *East Indians* to distinguish them from the native American Indians. In some parts of California, they are also referred to as Hindus (Leonard, 1993). In this book, I have referred to immigrants from the Indian sub-continent as *South Asians* and from Hong Kong and mainland China as *Chinese*, and the group as a whole as *Asians*.

Acknowledgements

I wish to thank my colleagues at the University of Wales at Aberystwyth for their help and support: in particular, Richard Daughtery for the sabbatical leave, Bob Jones for looking after the degree courses, and Gareth Elwyn Jones and Gerran Thomas for their moral support. I am very appreciative of the help I have received from Richard Lloyd and Daniel Chandler in reading through the manuscript with great care and making valuable suggestions. I am also indebted to those of my students who voluntarily read through some parts of the manuscript and evaluated their contents. Nevertheless, any errors or omissions remain my sole responsibility.

I found that the continuous and sustained effort needed to produce this manuscript became very absorbing and, on occasions, almost obsessive. I wish to thank my wife, Theresa, for not only putting up with me, but for also providing active support.

Copyright acknowledgements

Preface: Extract from *Anita and Me* by Meera Syal. © 1996 Meera Syal reprinted by kind permission of HarperCollins Publishers Ltd. and by the author c/o Rogers, Coleridge & White Ltd., 20 Powis Mews, London W11 1JN.

Chapter 2: Extract from *The Enigma of Arrival* by V. S. Naipaul. © 1987 V. S. Naipaul reprinted by kind permission of Gillon Aitken Associates Ltd.

Table 2.1: Adapted from Rose, E. B. J. and Deakin, N. (1969). *Colour and Citizenship: A report on British race relations.* Adapted by kind permission of Oxford University Press.

Table 3.1: Adapted from Roberts, H. and Sachdev, D. (1996). *Young People's Social Attitudes: Having their say – the views of 12- to 19-year-olds.* Adapted by kind permission of Barnardos.

Figure 3.2: Adapted from Modood, T., Berthoud, R., Lakey, J., Nazroo, J., Smith, P., Virdee, S. and Beishon, S. (1997). *Ethnic Minorities in Britain: Diversity and Disadvantage.* Adapted by kind permission of the Policy Studies Institute.

1

Introduction

Most parents and teachers in the 'Western world' are well aware of the pains and pleasures experienced by adolescents. Witness the popularity of books such as Sue Townsend's *The Diaries of Adrian Mole* and the regular feature article *Treasure* in *The Guardian*. Young people are prone to assert their individuality and question – even challenge – the authority of their parents on such matters as keeping their room tidy, playing loud music, hair styles, wearing fashionable clothes, types of friends (especially of the opposite sex) and staying up late. Increasingly, parents are worried about the use of drugs by young people, and would like to keep a close eye on their youngsters' friends and their social activities. As they approach mid-adolescence (15–16 years of age), there is an increasing concern over their schooling, education and vocational choices. Are they going to stay on after 16? What sort of jobs and careers are they aiming to pursue? These are some of the problems which both parents and their teenage sons and daughters have to face and which can cause considerable inter-generational tension and anxiety.

Theories of adolescence

Early theories of adolescence put forward the view that puberty is a period of great emotional and social upheaval. However, recent research (Coleman and Hendry, 1989) suggests that the vast majority of young people pass through this stage without major turmoil. But there are major physiological and cognitive changes during puberty which significantly affect young people's emotional moods, self-image and social relationships. The role expectations of parents and society are often diverse, and 'peer culture' – often with opposing values to those of the family – has a fascination for most young people. All in all, the internal body changes and external social pressures can make this period of development taxing and problematic.

Young people around the age of 14 years begin to ask questions relating to their identity: Who am I? What sort of person would I like to be? Erikson's writings (1968) on identity formation and identity crisis, from childhood through adolescence to adulthood and old age, shed some light on the predicament of young people. His theoretical model is essentially derived from the Freudian school of psychology but includes a social dimension and is highly conjectural. However, Marcia (1994) has operationalized his theoretical concepts into testable forms. There is little evidence, apart from his clinical cases, to support the model's validity, but it has its merits. His theory states that young people explore and experiment with their inner feelings and engage in independent thinking and acting because they undergo rapid physiological and mental development.

The positive outcome of this engagement (the formation of a *coherent identity*) depends upon how far the adolescent puts his or her trust in others, whether they make productive use of their energies and whether, and how far, they are being led by a realistic time perspective (that is, planning for the future and retaining a sense of time). Conversely, failure to accomplish these imperatives can lead to identity confusion (*identity diffusion*). Some young people, through loss of (or a lack of) a sense of coherent identity might choose a negative identity, and engage in anti-social activities such as gang fights, mugging, petty thieving and burglaries. Another important point in Erikson's theory is that the processes of formation of personal and social identities are complementary – that being 'at home' in one's body, in one's physical home and in one's social world all together are the keys to personal and social wellbeing. Whether his model is useful for understanding the life crisis of adolescents in other than an European context is a moot point which will be taken up in this book.

Personal and social identity

The quest for personal and social identity for British-born Asian young people (second/third generation) can be fraught with more difficulties than for their white counterparts. This is because of the deep gulf between certain values and social conventions of the home on the one hand, and of school and the wider society on the other. The first generation Asians, who migrated to Britain during the 1950s and 1960s, are (and were) very secure in their identities: these were rooted in their religion and family and kinship values (Stopes-Roe and Cochrane, 1990; Hutnik, 1991). There was little ambivalence on this matter. However, for the second generation, the process can be very painful indeed because of the conflicting demands made by home and school on their behaviour, loyalties and obligations.

In the USA and Canada, for instance, 'hyphenated' identities are acceptable and indeed widely used for various ethnic groups. It is a matter of pride for Americans of Chinese origin to call themselves 'Chinese-American' and likewise, in Canada, for people of Indian origin to be referred to as 'Indo-Canadians'. However, this notion of 'hyphenated identity' has never caught the imagination of the British public. Asian immigrants and their UK-born children are simply referred to as Asians (for Indians, Bangladeshis and Pakistanis) or by a derogatory term, such as *Pakis*. Immigrants of Chinese origin are usually referred to as Chinese, or by derogatory terms such as *Chinky* or *Slanty-Eyes*. However, some young Asian people who were born and educated in Britain do use such terms as 'British-Muslims' to describe themselves, while others refer to themselves more plainly as Indian or Pakistani, but the majority are content or feel easier using 'British' to describe their nationality rather than their way of life or cultural affinity. A comment of a Hindu boy from a study shows the unease of some young people:

I don't feel myself English, no not at all. I don't think I could. . . . I could make myself think that I'm English, but I don't think I could ever be English. I could be English in certain matters, but that doesn't mean that I think like I'm English.
(Taylor, 1976, p. 55)

In contrast to these examples, there are some ethnic young people who see the exposure to two cultures (through being bi-cultural and bilingual) as an opportunity to enrich their lives by developing new idioms for self-expression. For instance, there is an emergence of new tunes and rhythms in music which are derived from a mixture of *Bhangra*, *Rock* and *Reggae* musical traditions. Likewise, there have been innovations in food preparation and fashion clothes which combine strands from both Western and Eastern traditions. Simon Rattle, the conductor of the Birmingham Symphony Orchestra, has shown an innovative approach to classical music and is a leading light in expounding the musical traditions of Eastern cultures. There are some modern writers (such as Hanif Kureishi, Salman Rushdie and V.S. Naipaul) who have exploited inter-cultural tensions (both positives and negatives) to enrich the contemporary literary scene.

Researchers in the US (Phinney, 1996; 1990) and in Australia (Rosenthal, 1987) concluded from their studies that the majority of ethnic minority students think that their bi-culturalism confers on them many advantages which they can use to develop their self-expression and their abilities. However, it is important to note a caveat to these optimistic conclusions: the advantages of bilingualism and bi-culturalism are only likely to materialize in a society whose institutions tolerate, or indeed promote, cultural diversity. These issues of bi-culturalism will be explored later by using modern theories of acculturation, notably that of Berry's (1997). His model employs a social psychological perspective and has been used in many cultural settings.

Schooling

Subsequent generations of Asians are likely to face more difficulties and challenges in British/European schools than their white peers because of the fundamental differences between some of the values and social conventions of the schools and those of Asian homes. These include a clear role differentiation between boys and girls, an emphasis on religious observances and the primacy of the family's interest over that of the individual. It may be useful to illustrate the anxieties of parents and young people with a few verbatim extracts from interviews and case studies undertaken by researchers in this field. A Muslim father's view on mixed schooling highlights some of the problems:

My own view is they should not be mixed schools. I am in favour of separate schools. Kids begin to go wrong in their adolescent years. Our people are compelled to send them to mixed schools; there should be a choice. I know a lot of Muslim parents who feel this way.
(Ghuman, 1994, p. 105)

And the comment of a white head teacher is relevant:

. . . among the girls there is this whole business of getting back home and getting back safe so there is very little drama, music, dance they take part in and that's a shame.
(Parker-Jenkins, 1995, p. 94)

The majority of Muslim parents object to 'mixed' schooling (see Anwar, 1994; Ashraf, 1988) because of Islamic teaching which forbids the free mixing of boys and girls during puberty. There are also some Hindu and Sikh parents (for that matter there are a few indigenous whites too) who express their anxieties about the wide-spread indiscipline in co-educational schools and the *laissez-faire* attitude of schoolteachers on matters appertaining to dating and sex-related issues. A Sikh parent, who is also a home-school teacher, made a telling point:

In Vancouver schools they are putting condom machines, this has really frightened a lot of parents. Parents are scared to send their girls to school dances and other out-of-school activities because of drugs and promiscuous sex . . . I feel I would have done the same if I were not in the school system. Parent's fears are quite genuine.
(Ghuman, 1994, p. 87)

Chinese parents in the UK are far more flexible than Muslim and Sikh parents on these matters, but they too are concerned over indiscipline in schools. A Chinese-origin researcher in Manchester, England, found that parents think the main cause of indiscipline is the informal manners of teachers:

In Hong Kong we are taught about politeness and manners. Children respect their parents and they look after their elders. It is a different story in the UK. They even call their parents and uncles by their names . . . Anyway, it's our custom and I don't think school will accept our norms. So I have to be very strict with my children.
(Wong, 1987, p. 45)

Home–school conflicts

The differences between the general ethos of the Asian home and that of the school do create problems for young people (Drury, 1991). Asian families tend to be dominated by fathers who often use their position of authority to make decisions for the whole family, although there is a considerable variation within this social practice since factors such as religion, social class and the place of origin of the family have an important bearing. On the other hand, schools in Britain and North America are run mainly along democratic principles where students are encouraged to think for themselves and their viewpoints are given due recognition. Overall, schools attempt to develop autonomy in their students, whereas, at home, young people often have to learn to defer to the views of their parents and elders. A white deputy headmistress summed it up succinctly:

We teach girls to be independent and critical thinkers, but at home they are taught the virtues of collective responsibility and unquestioning respect to the elders in the family.
(Ghuman, 1994, p. 97)

Teachers' perceptions (sometimes stereotypes) of Asian parents also add to the difficulties of young people. Some white teachers, for instance, think that Asian parents are not really interested in their daughters' education. While this is the case with some parents, the majority do wish them to stay on for further education, albeit in single-sex institutions. It must be stressed that there are very wide variations among the different religious and ethnic groups on these matters and these are further compounded by South Asian class and caste (*varna*) differences.

In general, the attitudes of white teachers to the bilingualism (for example, Indo-English) of their Asian students are not very sympathetic (Verma and Ashworth, 1986). For instance, most white teachers are unsympathetic to the teaching of community languages and put their emphasis on anglicization and hence assimilation (absorption into the use of English) of their Asian students. A white headmaster's comment reflects a not untypical attitude:

What these kids [meaning Asians] *need is more practice in English not in Urdu. They ought to speak English at home, listen to the radio and read English books. This is the only way they can achieve higher academic standards. They might have a reasonable command of the spoken English, but they need to work at their written English. Also they should learn the British history and way of life.*
(Ghuman, 1995a, p. 38–39)

This is a well-meaning comment which tends to underline the traditional role of schools as purveyors of middle-class British values and culture. Some working-class white parents also sense such an attitude from teachers and become defensive and alienated from school. This type of situation creates a further gulf between home and school, and will more than likely exacerbate inter-generational tension and anxiety.

Prejudice

Racial prejudice is a fact of life for many Asian and black families in Britain (see Jones, 1993; Milner, 1983; Davey, 1983) . Proportionally more Asian children and youngsters have been the victim of bullying than their white peers; and some white teachers, albeit unintentionally, are also racially prejudiced (DES: Swann Report, 1985; Verma *et al.*, 1994) To overcome this disadvantage, many young people anglicize their names and many parents send their children to public fee-paying schools to improve their accents and general confidence (Ghuman, 1994). (Helweg and Helweg (1990) also found this practice of anglicizing names amongst people of Indian subcontinent origin in the US.) An example of how upsetting racial prejudice is for Asian people is provided by a father of Chinese origin:

Racial discrimination is very serious in our area. People living here are mostly on the dole. They throw stones at our chip shop . . . I won't allow my daughter to go out on her own, not even for swimming, in case some English throw her into the water . . . I am always asked: Why do you come here and take our money away?
(Wong, 1987, p. 45)

The following extract from an American study reveals the extent of racial prejudice in American high schools:

Father: *With the American children. They hate our children. They keep on calling 'Hindu, Hindu' . . . Secondly, pulling off someone's turban, or spitting, this is really bad . . . He was very upset.*
Son: *Everyone has their turbans off. Most boys have had their hair cut.*
[Sikhs are not supposed to cut their hair.]
(Gibson, 1988, p. 143; *author's parentheses*)

Children become aware of their own racial origin as early as the age of five years old and soon after begin to attach positive and/or negative feelings to their own and other children's ethnicity (Davey, 1983). In secondary school, friendship patterns of youngsters are largely influenced by their ethnicity.

Incidents of racial harassment of Asian pupils by their white peers in both primary and secondary schools have been found by many researchers (Kelly and Cohen, 1988; CRE, 1987). Regrettably, some white teachers are not immune from this charge. A quotation from a study shows how some Asian young people develop strategies to accommodate to their teachers' prejudice:

You try to humour them [teachers] *. . . they treat you as though you are from another planet or something. If you get on well with them they stop hating you . . . but you have to try first. If you start putting a barrier between them and you, they hate you more, so you have always got to try to be your best side for them.*
(Verma and Ashworth, 1986, p. 125)

Some researchers (Troyna and Hatcher, 1992) have argued that Asian students, in general, do not complain about the racial prejudice they encounter from their teachers because they do not wish to upset their parents unduly. Gibson (1988), who has carried out a number

7

of studies on the social adjustment and educational achievement of Asian and other ethnic minority students in the USA, writes:

> *When questioned specifically about whether some teachers were biased, Punjabi students said they did not think so. Informal interviews with high school teachers and staff revealed, however, a strong and unmistakable undercurrent of prejudice.*
> (Gibson, 1988, p. 150)

Unemployment

The unemployment rate among Asian (and indeed West Indian) young people is often twice as high as that of their white counterparts in some regions of the UK (Jones, 1993). The first generation had a similar experience but they accepted this situation as it was generally thought that their vocational skills were not comparable to those of their white counterparts and their command of the English language was very poor. However, there is substantial research evidence (Modood *et al.*, 1997; Brown, 1985; Smith, 1977) to show that second generation skilled and professional young people, who have gained their qualifications from British universities and higher colleges of education, are still discriminated against by employers in favour of indigenous whites. The racism which is entrenched in the structures of British institutions (such as the Law, Police, Civil Service and the Armed Forces) can have a demoralizing effect on the morale of Asian young people. There is a growing body of psychological literature which helps us to understand and, hopefully, combat, racial prejudice and counteract its effect on children and young people. A discussion on this topic will be taken up in *Chapters 3* and *4*.

To adjust to the differing expectations of home and school, many young people develop their own unique ways of coping, for example, by compartmentalizing their behaviour (Wade and Souter, 1992). Asian girls have been found to reconcile the conflicting demands in 'dressing' for school by keeping their tights and other accessories in their lockers. They come to school in their traditional clothes and change into school 'dress' in the toilets before reverting to their traditional dress to go home.

Home–school convergence

Although emphasis has been placed chiefly on the *differences* between home and school, there are many areas where the values of the two institutions do converge remarkably. Asian parents perceive education as a means of social mobility and are prepared to make both financial and personal sacrifices to see their children succeed. There is evidence in the literature to show that Asian young people, with the exception of Bangladeshis (see Gillborn and Gipps, 1996), are achieving as well as, or even better than, their white peers in Britain and North America (Gillborn and Gipps, 1996; Ogbu, 1994; Gibson, 1988). Also in general, parents respect teachers and value their moral and social support. Furthermore, most Asian parents are extremely hardworking and instil this habit of industry and persistence in their children. In practice, it means that parents encourage their children to work diligently at school, do their homework regularly, respect their teachers and stay on for further and higher education. These matters are examined in *Chapter 5*.

Dating

Another major area of inter-generational conflict in Asian homes stems from when their young people, like their white peers, start to take an interest in adolescents of the opposite sex. This is considered quite normal and healthy by white British parents, but Asian parents generally disapprove of (and some are strongly against) this social practice, particularly when their daughters are involved. Most of the marriages in rural India, Pakistan and Hong Kong are arranged by the family and this social custom is still considered very important by Asians in this country. Asian parents are prone to put more restrictions on their daughters than on their sons, and this can be a cause of some resentment and even anger as Gibson (1988) noted with Sikh youths in California. A girl talks about her parents' reactions to her lifestyle:

My parents don't like my clothes, my hair, the way I talk. They don't like my future plans. They don't like anything about me. They don't like my philosophy about marriage. You should marry an East Indian [meaning of Indian origin] *... But my parents say, 'Don't talk to anybody; don't go anywhere; come straight home.' And that's it.*
(Gibson, 1988, p. 135, author's words in parentheses)

The practice of dating affects girls far more than boys because most parents tend to turn a blind eye if their own boys are involved. Traditionally, girls are thought to carry the honour of the family and of the kinship group. Furthermore, Asian parents, in general, think that in Western societies women are 'sexually exploited' and, therefore, their daughters need a strict upbringing to counteract the effect of

9

the liberal regime of schools and that of the wider society. It is not surprising to find that most Asian parents – and, of course, many white parents – are more protective of their daughters and treat them differently. They tend to be more strict with them on matters relating to dress, hairstyle, household chores and general 'independence'. There is evidence (Drury, 1991; Dosanjh and Ghuman, 1996) to suggest that some parents also favour their sons when giving out pocket money and buying books and other material things and when excusing them from help with household chores. More importantly, there is a tendency among most parents (Hindu parents are an exception to this) to give more encouragement to boys to stay on for further and higher education. This can be a source of grievance among girls. A Muslim girl gave a candid account of this situation:

But what I'm trying to say is it's only the minority who are like you [meaning have freedom and can go to college]. *Most of the girls I know aren't allowed to go out after school. I know I ain't and a few friends, quite a lot of them, aren't allowed to do that. It's only, you know, a few people, that I know are in . . . situation here and that it's well I think it's wrong. We should be allowed some amount of, . . . like, we need to get socialised, we need to . . . go out once a day and, you know, see what the world around us is like.*
(Wade and Souter, 1992, p. 39–40)

It is tempting to say that British-born Asian young adolescents should enjoy the same rights as their white counterparts do and that it is a question of human rights for girls to be treated equally. Whilst legally and morally this may be an appropriate stance to take, it has wider and serious ramifications for the survival of the Asian family and kinship. Most Asian parents face the following dilemma: how much freedom are they going to allow their daughters? This is a complex matter which requires a fuller understanding of the religious and cultural imperatives of the different Asian groups. As an illustration of the situation, consider the response of an Indo-Canadian father:

Teachers say to our daughters your parents are your jailers! This they justify on human rights. But we can't give up all our customs. Our survival is at stake. We think the best for our children and families – not for our own ego.
(Ghuman, 1994, p. 97)

The failure of parents to understand and appreciate the anxieties of growing young people lies partly, at least, in the outlook and attitudes of Asian parents who themselves are predominantly from a rural background. Their own adolescence was short and relatively painless. Most of the first generation parents, after leaving primary and/or middle school, went to work on their family farms or took up the trades of their parents and accepted arranged marriages. Decisions on their work and 'love' lives (two major and difficult decisions to make in the Western world) were taken by their parents and they had little say on these matters. These issues are explored in the pages that follow by using concepts from a variety of psychological theories and interdisciplinary perspectives.

Summary

Young people of Asian origin in Britain, North America and Australia face special problems of adjustment during adolescence because of the conflict of values and social mores between home and the wider society. To use the Eriksonian framework, it may be conjectured that many young people, especially girls, are likely to face an 'identity crisis' because of the very different expectations of the family and the school. The development of coherent identity is likely to be facilitated only if there is a symbiotic relationship between home and school. On the other hand, if young people receive conflicting messages from these institutions and thus diverse emotional and social demands and commitments are made, they are likely to be confused in their identity.

There is a substantial body of research which suggests that UK-born Asian youngsters, despite their British schooling and qualifications, face racial prejudice and discrimination – as did their fore-fathers/ mothers – in employment and, indeed, in all walks of life (Modood *et al.*, 1997). Such a situation is not likely to encourage the integration of new generations into the British way of life and culture. On the other hand, it may be argued that the feelings of rejection thus engendered may cause frustration and aggression, which in turn can lead to 'separation' tendencies, and some youths may be alienated both from 'home' and societal cultures.

In the next chapter, the backgrounds of the first generation Asian immigrants (people from the Indian sub-continent, South Asians and Chinese mainly from Hong Kong) are discussed in such a way that inter-generational tensions and anxieties can be placed within their wider social and cultural contexts. *Chapter 3* examines in some detail the extent and degree (in nature and development) of racial prejudice against young Asians in Britain, by employing a variety of psychological perspectives (Allport, 1954; Jones, 1997). Also, gender-related issues are examined in the light of research, and young people's concerns over such matters as dating and arranged marriages are brought into focus for discussion. *Chapter 4* explores the issues relating to the development and measurement of ethnic identity in the light of various psychological theories. The up-to-date research on 'acculturation' (Berry, 1997) is presented and its relevance to young peoples' lives is discussed in some detail. In *Chapter 5*, the roles of school and teachers in promoting ethnic relationships are explored. In addition, matters relating to cognitive styles, scholastic achievement and the special concerns of Asian girls are discussed in the light of recent research. In the last chapter, an attempt is made to synthesize the main points of the book and it concludes by advocating some positive measures which may help the situation of British-born young people of Asian ancestry.

Further reading

Anwar, M. (1994). *Young Muslims in Britain*. Leicester: The Islamic Foundation.
A readable introductory text on the concerns of Muslim youth in the UK.

Coleman, C.J. and Hendry, L. (1989). *The Nature of Adolescence*. London: Routledge.
A useful general book on adolescence.

Gibson, M.A. (1988). *Accommodation Without Assimilation: Sikh Immigrants in an American High School*. Ithaca, NY and London: Cornell University Press.
Readers who wish to broaden their knowledge on this topic are strongly recommended to look at Chapters 1 and 3 of this lucidly written book. It is based on fieldwork in California.

Pan, L. (1991). *Sons of the Yellow Emperor: The story of the overseas Chinese*. London: Secker and Warburg.
A readable general introduction to Chinese communities overseas.

Parker, D. (1994). *The Chinese in Britain: Annotated bibliography and research resources*. Coventry: Centre for Research in Ethnic Relations, University of Warwick.

Parker, D. (1995). *Through Different Eyes: The cultural identities of young Chinese people in Britain*. Aldershot: Avebury.
The first few chapters are rather difficult (quite a lot of jargon) and may be omitted on the first reading. Chapters 5, 6, and 7 are clearly written and informative.

Stopes-Roe, M. and Cochrane, R (1990). *Citizens of this Country: The Asian-British*. Clevedon: Multilingual Matters.
Research-based book on young people (18- to 21-year olds) of Indian and Pakistani origin. The fieldwork was carried out in Birmingham, UK. It is very informative on research methods used in social psychology.

Wade, B. and Souter, P. (1992). *Continuing to Think: The British Asian girl*. Clevedon: Multilingual Matters.
The title is somewhat misleading because the study is based on a small sample of Muslim girls only – nevertheless a readable account.

2

First Generation: Religion, Value Orientations and Gender Issues

I was his opposite in every way, social, artistic, sexual. And considering that his family's fortune had grown, but enormously, with the spread of the empire in the nineteenth century, it might be said that an empire lay between us. The empire in the end at the same linked us. This empire explained my birth in the New World, the language I used, the vocation and ambition I had; this empire in the end explained my presence there in the valley, in that cottage, in the grounds of the manor. But we were – or had started – at opposite ends of wealth, privilege, and in the hearts of different cultures.
(Naipaul, 1987, p. 174)

The aims of this chapter are twofold: to describe the social and religious backgrounds of the first generation of Asians who migrated to Britain after the Second World War, and to show how their values and attitudes directly influenced the relationship between them and their adolescents. The Asian people included in this study are those from the Indian sub-continent (India, Pakistan and Bangladesh) and those of Chinese extraction, mainly from Hong Kong.

The migration of Asian people to Britain should be placed within the broader context of the mass-scale movement of people from developing countries to Western European countries since the Second World War. According to Cohen (1991, p.15), 'By the mid-1970s, when immigration restrictions were imposed in all Western countries, some 13.5 million foreigners were officially counted as residing in Belgium, Denmark . . . the UK, Sweden and Switzerland'.

Immigration to the UK

There were only a small number of Asians in the UK before the
Second World War: Desai (1963) puts the number at around fifteen
thousand. This number consisted mainly of seamen (also called
lascars), who jumped ship and moved inland to work in city factories;
doctors, and students who stayed on after the completion of their
studies (Rose and Deakin, 1969, p. 70). The number of immigrants
increased significantly during the 1960s as there were employment
opportunities in transport, in clothing manufacturing industries in
the North, in heavy steel industry in the English Midlands, and in
a rubber factory in Southall, a borough of London. The Chinese and
Bangladeshi immigrants had their main employment in family-run
restaurant businesses in the big cities. Until 1962, entry to the UK
by Commonwealth citizens was voluntarily controlled by the 'sending
countries' (India, Pakistan, West Indies and Hong Kong) in restricting
the issue of passports. Thereafter it was controlled through the 'work
voucher' scheme, which meant that an intending immigrant had to
obtain a voucher from the British High Commissioner in his/her
home country A number of subsequent Acts of Parliament tightened
immigration even further (see Fryer, 1984). *Table 1.1* shows the Asian
immigrant population as it stood in 1966.

The passing of the 1971 Immigration Act (which actually came
into force in 1973) ended virtually all primary immigration from the
Commonwealth countries. Only the wives and children of men who
had settled permanently in the UK were considered, and they were
allowed in only after a very thorough scrutiny. The latest census
data available, from 1991 (Owen, 1992), shows that the total number
of people from the Indian sub-continent is nearly one and a half
million and those of Chinese origin number one hundred and fifty
seven thousand – 2.7 and 0.3 per cent, respectively, of the British
population.

Another source of major Asian migration was from the East African
countries. During the 1970s, many thousands of British Asians
(holding British passports) were forced to leave their homes in
Uganda – mainly for political reasons (many were expelled by Idi

*Table 2.1: Estimates of Asians in England and Wales 1966 (adapted from
Rose and Deakin, 1969, p. 97).*

Indian	163,600
Pakistani (including Bangladesh)	67,700
Far Eastern (Hong Kong, Malaya, and Singapore)	47,000

Amin), and a selected number were allowed entry to the UK. Others went to Canada and Australia. These immigrants generally had a higher level of education, greater entrepreneurial skills and were more anglicized compared with the people from the Indian sub-continent and, consequently, they found it easier to integrate into the British way of life. Indeed, the most recent Policy Studies Institute survey (Modood *et al.*, 1997) found this group of South Asians and Chinese to be faring nearly as well as the white population in education, housing and employment.

It is important to note, however, that the vast majority of Asian immigrants were from the middle-strata of their communities and from rural backgrounds. It was chiefly the well-off families who could afford the expensive air fares and payments to agents and other officials to ease the issue of passports (sometimes illegal) and other relevant papers. The main motive of the earlier immigrants (who were invariably single men and sojourners) was economic, that is, they wanted to earn enough money in the UK to improve their family's standard of living back home.

Watson (1975) has extensively studied Chinese immigrants from the New Territories in Hong Kong. His comments are revealing as to the main objective of the immigrants:

Many immigrants buy land with their savings but an equally attractive investment is to build 'sterling houses' (named after the remittances that pay for their construction) . . . Yet, by building in the New Territories the owner believes he will always be able to return to a comfortable home in a secure social environment after retirement'.
(Watson, 1975, p. 208)

According to Watson, they considered their stay in Britain to be a short-term one and hoped to return home to enjoy the benefits of their hard work. This myth of return has been sustained by very many immigrants all over the world, who feel that one day they will return to their country of origin, but very few realize it due to a variety of complex reasons. Anwar (1979) illustrates this myth vividly by discussing the case of Pakistanis who initially came to the UK for three to five years, but who, with the exception of very few, have now permanently settled in the UK with their families. He concludes his research on the first generation:

Many wish to go back but in reality economic circumstances are such that the majority are unlikely ever to return. There is also a

possibility that the cultural and familial bonds with Pakistan may weaken with the second generation.
(Anwar, 1979, p. 222)

In all probability, the decision by Asians to settle permanently has been due mainly to the imposition of restrictions on immigration, the better employment opportunities and the general benefit of living in the UK with its highly developed welfare, national health and education systems. The reader should appreciate that Asians comprise people from many diverse religious, cultural and regional backgrounds and, in order to maintain solidarity with kin-groups, have settled in enclaves (ghettos) which are mostly in inner-city areas of the UK. Thus, Chinatowns in Manchester, Liverpool and London are well known, as is the enclave of Sikhs and Hindus in Southall, a suburb of London (sometimes referred to as 'the little Punjab'), and that of Muslims in Bradford, Yorkshire.

Religious and cultural backgrounds of South Asians (Indian sub-continent)

In order to fully understand the concerns and anxieties of contemporary Asian adolescents, it is important to appreciate the religious and cultural values of the first generation immigrants. Immigrants from the Indian sub-continent belong to three main religions, namely Hindu, Sikh and Muslim, although there are also a small number of Christians and Bhuddists. The majority of people from India belong to the Sikh and Hindu faiths, whereas immigrants from Pakistan and Bangladesh are Muslim.

Hinduism

Hinduism is an ancient religion, over 2,000 years old (see Sen, 1961), and there are very many strands and schisms within it. It is polytheistic, and is a tolerant religion which has learned to adapt in some degree to survive the impact of Islam and Christianity, both of which have a clear-written theology and dogmas, and which, furthermore, were the religions of the conquering invaders. There are *three* central notions of the Hindu religion: *karma* (both good and bad actions have their consequences, both in this life and the after-life – the law of cause and effect); *dharma* (duty and commitment); and a belief in the reincarnation of the soul. The supreme aim of this life is to attain *Nirvana/Moksha* (a lasting blissful release from the pains and anguish of 84 *lakhs* (births and deaths)) by heeding one's *karma* and *dharma*. The Hindu theology is multifarious, therefore Hinduism is more a way of life than a dogma-led religion. Jackson and Nesbitt (1993) describe it succinctly as: 'Hinduism is an umbrella term for a great number of practices and beliefs each of which belongs to some of the millions of people of India who for historical reasons are called Hindus.' There are many rituals which govern the preparation and serving of food, for example (*suchha* – pure and *judha* – impure) and fasting.

The caste rituals of purification are important to the Hindus. Their caste (*varna*) system was devised by Manu (Nehru, 1946) and was originally based on a hierarchy of occupational structure. The upper-class consisted of people who were principally to be concerned with religious and scholarly matters(*brahmins*); the category below was that of warriors and protectors of society (*kashsytrias*); then followed the *vaishsa*, the farmers and herdsmen; and, lastly, the caste of *lagis* (barbers, weavers, carpenters, blacksmiths). The lowest caste (*shudras*) were to do the dirty and menial jobs of cleaning lavatories and public places and the like (hence the name 'untouchables'). According to the traditional customs of the Hindus, the untouchables were to be excluded from all civic, religious and political activities. Although these practices were outlawed in the Indian constitution in January, 1949, their heinous effect is still to be found in many walks of life in modern India.

The Sikh religion

The Sikh religion was founded by Guru Nank (1469 A.D. to 1539 A.D.), who was of Hindu origin but abhorred the pernicious effect of the caste system and the oppression exercised by brahmins over the masses through the imposition of myriads of meaningless religious rites and ceremonial rituals. Unlike the people of his own creed, he believed and preached the existence of 'One God' (*Aik Ongkar*, see Singh, 1966) and the unity of mankind. The Sikh religion was later militarized by the tenth Guru (Gobind Singh), who prescribed a code of conduct and dress for his followers, one of the salient principles of which was not to cut one's hair and to wear a turban, which subsequently became the distinguishing feature of the Sikhs. Sikhs are prohibited to smoke and drink and should, strictly speaking, be vegetarians. The younger generation, however, both in India and abroad, are becoming very lax in all these principles, especially in the wearing of a turban over their uncut hair.

Despite the recent tensions in the Punjab, Hindu and Sikh communities still share and celebrate a number of common festivals (Diwali, Holy), both in India and the UK, and intermarriages between the two communities are not uncommon. I will discuss Asian marriage systems in more detail presently, but suffice it to say at this stage that caste (and *varna* – sub-caste) is the most important consideration in arranging marriages amongst Hindus, Sikhs and Muslims. The saliency of caste has been observed by Nesbitt (1998) in a recent study of Hindu and Sikh young people in the English Midlands: 'Ethnographic research . . . suggests a complex situation in which caste membership is integral to identity and situationally significant for both Gujaratis and Punjabis, whether Sikh or Hindu'.

The Muslim religion

The Muslim religion is strictly monotheistic and has a strong antipathy towards the Hindu custom of idolatry. The prophet Mohammed, the founder of Islam, strictly forbade idol worship and preached submission to Allah and the conduct of everyday life according to prescribed religious principles. Islam embodies a total way of life and its followers believe they will achieve inner harmony and peace in this life and happiness in the life to come. The spiritual, moral and social principles of living and worshipping are to be found in the Koran, the holy book of the Muslims, which was revealed to the Prophet Mohammed in the seventh century. It is written in Arabic and all devout Muslims are expected to learn to recite it by heart. All believers must embody the following five principles in their lives: a belief that there is no god but Allah; that Mohammed is Allah's messenger; the reciting of five compulsory daily prayers; the payment of *zakah* (welfare contribution); and fasting during Ramadan. As in other religions, there are multifarious interpretations of the teaching of the Holy Koran and this has led to the formation of many sects, movements and schisms within the world-wide Muslim community. Thus, the varying interpretations of Koranic teaching have been used to support the most 'liberal' style of life (such as full equality of women with men in education and employment) as well as to justify the creed of fundamentalism, which forbids the meeting of men and women in public and applies the strict *shria* law; for example, stoning to death for adultery and the amputation of limbs for theft. The different religious sects and creeds within the Islamic faith have found their expression in the burgeoning of local mosques – estimated to be around 1,000 in the UK. The mosque has become a centre for the religious, educational and political activities of Muslim communities, and *imams* (priests, also sometimes referred to as *mullahs*) of mosques often have a strong influence on the way parents rear and educate their children and how they treat their growing adolescents. A headmaster of a multicultural school described the role of a *mullah*:

Most parents in my school would be happy to leave it to the staff. But the older generation of leaders within the mosque – very

encapsulated and in a narrow Islamic tradition – had a strong
influence on the local Muslim community. Parents of the sixties
were persuaded to ask for a mullah [priest] *to be in the school.*
Lurking behind this worry lies this unease that their children are
being corrupted; and this is not too strong a word.
(Ghuman, 1996, p. 68)

The building of mosques, Gurudwaras (a Sikh place of worship)
and temples in the UK provided the immigrants with an institution
which helped them maintain their distinctive religious and social
identities and indeed the way of life which they brought with them
(no value judgement is intended here). Religion plays, and has
played, an important role in the lives of the first generation of
Indians, Pakistanis and Bangladeshis, more so with Muslims and
Sikhs than with Hindus. Muslim communities in the UK are far
more united and vociferous in their demands than those of other
immigrants. Many Muslim parents would prefer separate schools
for their girls and they want several changes made to the curriculum
of the school, especially in the domain of religious education, the
teaching of physical education, music and drama (see Anwar, 1996;
1998). (These issues will be discussed in *Chapter 5*.)

The religious and family backgrounds of Chinese immigrants

Most of the first generation Chinese immigrants from Hong Kong
believed in their traditional religion, which is a mixture of ancestral
worship, polytheism and superstition. These practices have influenced
Confucianism, Taoism and Buddhism, the three major religions of
Hong Kong, which in turn have had their effect in changing traditional
religious practices. Ancestral worship and celebration of festivals are
the two most important practices engaged in by the Chinese.

Confucianism

The philosophy of Confucius had a pervasive influence on the
Chinese psyche. According to one authoritative source:

His theories of government were not successful . . . However, the
teachings and way of life he had commended to his disciples lived
on, and were themselves to make an important and revolutionary
impact upon Chinese society . . . He was a religious and moral
reformer but he sought to reform religion through ethics rather
than ethics through religion.
(Smart, 1968, p. 196)

At the heart of Confucian philosophy are five relationships: those between father and son; between elder brother and younger; between husband and wife; between elders and the young; and between ruler and subject. Although the latter of each pair is deemed inferior in status to the former, these relationships were to be ordered according to appropriate dispositions (*li*) of both parties. For instance, the son should show filial piety and the father in turn should be kind – thus underlying the concept of reciprocity in human relationships. At the centre of Confucian philosophy is the primacy of relationships within the family which, properly conducted, would lead to true human welfare.

Taoism

Another source of influence on the Chinese personality has been Taoism. The basic principle of the Taoist ethic has been pithily expressed by Smart (1968): 'The mother of all, then, is a symbol of the power of passivity'. Such a principle advocates the naturalness of existence and the shunning of desires for wealth and prestige, a philosophy close to Buddhism, for one of the main tenets of Buddhist belief is the striving for *Nirvana* through meditation, self-denial and inner reflection. From the foregoing, it follows that Chinese worshipping practices can include strands from all these religious principles even when they might declare their allegiance to one specific creed, such as Buddhism.

The mixture of religious and cultural traditions has led to the evolving of a number of imperatives which have implications for the treatment and education of Chinese adolescents (Fong and Wu, 1996). It is held that young people should bring honour to the family, be respectful to the elders and be obedient to the older members of the family. Boys in the family are brought up to be high achievers, whereas girls are socialized to be virtuous women and to marry well. Chinese households 'even in modern cities with mixed cultures such as Singapore and Hong Kong, contain three or more generations in one living unit or close by one another,' according to Fong and Wu (*Ibid*, p. 73). Politeness and courtesy to elders at all times should invariably be part and parcel of young people's behaviour. Failure to observe these would bring shame and dishonour to the family.

Collective vs. individualistic orientation and Asian immigrants

Researchers have endeavoured to establish the differences in value systems, which affect attitude orientations, between modern and traditional societies. Kluckholn and Strodbeck (1961), taking an anthropological stance, have postulated differences between the two within five major dimensions. These appertain to:

- belief in 'human nature' – whether it is evil or good or a mixture of the two;
- 'the relationships between man and nature' – whether it is believed to be subjugation to nature, harmony with nature, or mastery over nature;
- 'evaluation of time perspectives' – an emphasis on time past, present or future;
- 'evaluation of the meaning of activity' – an emphasis on being, being in development, or an emphasis on doing; and, lastly;
- 'significant relationships' – to be governed by individual or collective considerations.

Collectivism

Whilst charting the differences between Asian immigrants and indigenous people can be informative in all five dimensions, the most productive and researched dimension, from a social and psychological perspective, is that of 'collectivity vs. individuality'. Let us define these concepts in some detail in order to work out the full implications for understanding the issues as these relate to inter-generational conflict and tension. Collectivism implies that an individual's thinking and behaviour are largely governed by the influence of a group to which he or she belongs; it could be the extended family, kinship or any other significant party. In the collectivist mode, achievements in life are principally viewed as bringing honour and glory to the family, a clan or a religious body. Fong and Wu (1996) have demonstrated that the real concern of traditional Chinese families, for instance, has been to enhance the honour of the clan and to glorify the ancestors through high achievement in one's studies and in business. Individuals in a group-conscious society are often called upon to make personal sacrifices to support their extended family which includes aunts, uncles, nephews, nieces and distant relatives. A comment of one researcher (Shaw, 1988) is illustrative of this situation:

In fact my disappointment arose from my own prejudices . . . from a western point of view, an individual who fulfils her or his role with the family, biraderi (kinship) and community, does so at the cost of individual freedom. However, most Pakistanis themselves, including the younger generation, do not see the matter in this way. They do not prize 'individuality' as high as westerners do,

and for most of them the sacrifice of 'individuality' that the
culture requires is more than offset by the advantages of fulfilling
one's role within the family, biraderi and community.
(Shaw, 1988, p. 128)

Individualism

Individualist orientation is the opposite of the collective. In such a value system, children from the early years are encouraged to develop autonomy, independent thinking, self-expression and achievement for themselves. The overall aim is to develop into inner-directed persons. Triandis (1994), the leading exponent of this model, concludes from his extensive researches that 'The basic findings, thus far, generally confirm Hofstede's contention that European-derived cultures are more individualistic than Asian or Latin American cultures, and that affluence, social mobility, and small family size are antecedents of individualism'. Likewise, Kim *et al.* (1994) argue that, in the West, liberalism serves as a foundation for individualism; on the other hand, in East Asian cultures, Confucianism serves as a moral-political philosophy that helps to entrench collectivism.

It is apposite at this point to mention that, although this conceptual framework does not imply any value judgement as to the superiority/inferiority of societies or individuals who engage in a lifestyle influenced by either collectivity or individuality, some critics (Kagitcibasi, 1997) argue that such a discourse does implicitly undermine and oversimplify the attributes of traditional societies. It is also contended that there is an enormous variation of behaviour within societies and that some individuals in a collectivist society could manifest both these styles. Despite these and other valid criticisms of this theory, I think it has its merit in helping us to understand some of the intergenerational concerns under discussion as will become clear in subsequent chapters.

Witkin and his associates (1966; 1975) have developed a holistic theory of personality and cognition in which notions of collectivity versus individuality are given a central position. According to the theory, group-oriented individuals tend to be *field-dependent* in their thinking and problem-solving styles, that is, they are led by the context in which information is given and are less prone to analyse and synthesize than are the *field-independent*. Furthermore, the former tend to conform to the prevailing social norms and are highly sensitive in picking up social cues. In personality, field-independent people use repression selectively, whereas the field dependent are more likely to repress indiscriminately, blotting out large chunks of their experiences willy-nilly without identifying the precise cause of their anxiety (Bertini, quoted in Fontana, 1988). Witkin *et al.* (1971) summarize the differences between the two types:

Thus, we consider it more differentiated if, in his perception of the world, the person perceives parts of the field as discrete and the field as structured . . . We consider it more differentiated if the person has a feeling as an individual distinct from others and has internalised, developed standards to guide his view of the world and himself.
(Witkin *et al.*, 1971)

The authors emphatically deny any value judgement associated with these modes of psychological functioning. Nevertheless, it has been found that people from settled farming communities (Berry, 1976; Vernon, 1969) are likely to exhibit a field-dependent style of functioning whereas people from Western societies are likely to be more field-independent. Although there are problems relating to the model's conceptual validity and lack of testing in cross-cultural contexts, such a holistic theory has some power in explaining the constellation of differences in personality and thinking styles between the offspring of Asians and their indigenous white counterparts. A further discussion on the cognitive styles of Asian young people is to be found in *Chapter 5*.

Arranged marriages and the position of women

In general, Asian people have stressed the significance and need for interdependence on the part of their family members, as opposed to rugged individualism. Asians tend to equate individualism with selfishness (Helweg and Helweg, 1990). The system of arranged marriages is but one example of this. The chief aim of arranged marriages is not to help realize the pleasure and happiness of the marrying couple, but to enhance the social prestige and economic circumstances of a family through an alliance with another family of equal or higher social status. The institution of marriage is still viewed, unlike in Western countries, as a regulator of 'sexuality' and valued for the stability and continuity it provides for the continuation of lineage. This practice is still common in India, Pakistan, Bangladesh and Hong Kong, especially in rural areas from where the vast majority of immigrants originated. 'Marriage was a family concern, not a private matter between man and wife. Choice of mates was based on considerations other than romantic love', writes

Sung (1967, p.153) in her description of Chinese customs. The overwhelming majority of the first generation had their marriages arranged by their parents or 'go-betweens' (see Shaw, 1988).

In general, there is a clear role differentiation between men and women, and between boys and girls in rural areas of Asia, although it is changing somewhat in urban areas. The woman's role is mainly confined to household duties and education for women is viewed in a far less favourable light. Women are the main carers of children and elderly parents which gives them an important supportive role in the family. In contrast, in the UK and elsewhere in Western countries, there has been a strong movement to secure an equality and parity of esteem of women with men. Consequently, this has been found to be one of the difficulties in the integration of Asian immigrants into the British way of life.

The first generation of Chinese families in the UK treated women as homemakers, a practice similar to that of their counterpart immigrants in the US. Sung (1967) describes the Chinese family scenario in America:

In the strictly first generation family, the father is the undisputed head of the household. He makes the decisions, manages the finances, and expects unquestioned obedience from both his wife and children ... the husband may hold the purse, but more likely than not, the wife will decide how its contents will be spent.
(Sung, 1967, p. 162)

Racial discrimination

The colonial legacy left its mark on the psyche of both rulers and ruled. Relationships between the immigrants and British white people were conducted, if somewhat implicitly, on the premise of superiority of the whites over the Asians. The full force of this racial prejudice was felt by the incoming immigrants in employment, housing, the schools where they sent their children and, indeed, in all walks of life (Rex and Tomlinson, 1979). Rose and Deakin write:

The hostility to the Sikhs arose not only from the overcrowding of houses and the way their houses seemed neglected; there was also resentment at success ... There were complaints of building of Gurudwaras and of the sounds of the ceremonies that issued from them.
(Rose and Deakin, p. 464)

Chinese people mostly found employment in family or kinship-run 'take-aways' and restaurants and therefore they were spared the worst aspects of racism (Watson, 1977). But still they encountered racial prejudice from customers.

The people from the Indian sub-continent were able to find jobs in factories and foundries which were not favoured by indigenous whites. Although they received equal wages, the niches which they occupied in the market were poor ones – dirty and unskilled jobs which required shift work and paid low wages. Even the qualified immigrants, such as teachers and engineers, found themselves working alongside their uneducated semi-skilled compatriots as their qualifications were not often recognized. Asian doctors were employed as a last resort when authorities could not recruit from indigenous qualified graduates, but even then mainly to work in the Casualty and Geriatric units (Anwar and Ali, 1987).

Similar examples of institutionalized racism and prejudice can be found in the teaching profession. The qualifications of most of the Asian teachers were not recognized by the then DES (Ranger, 1988; Ghuman, 1995a). Those who were lucky enough to achieve qualified status only found jobs in inner-city areas where there were a large number of Asian pupils.

Discrimination in the allocation of council housing was widespread as was the prejudice shown by white owners to intending Asian buyers. Stopes-Roe and Cochrane (1990) describe the situation in Birmingham (UK), as told to them by their respondents, 'Refuse to sell it to Asians in white areas, but are eager to sell in "ghetto" areas where whites don't want to buy'; 'white areas are impossible for us. The English leave when we have houses near them.'

Rex and Tomlinson (1979) carried out a comprehensive survey of the social and economic situation of Asian and West Indian immigrants in Handsworth, Birmingham, UK, and concluded:

The level of jobs occupied by West Indians and Asians, though it does overlap substantially with that of the white British living in the area, is in fact concentrated more in the lower reaches of the occupational system . . . Their houses, apart from the council houses which some of them live in, are the worst houses in the city which have not yet been demolished even though they are eligible for, and to some extent have benefited from, improvement grants. Their children go to primary and comprehensive schools which are largely segregated. Or are, at least, immigrant majority schools. In these schools they are held back by linguistic and cultural difficulties, to which teachers tend to react in terms of racial stereotypes.

(Rex and Tomlinson, 1979, p. 207)

This overall picture of the disadvantaged position of Asians vis-à-vis indigenous whites lasting into the mid-1980s is confirmed by the reports of the Policy Studies Institute (Smith, 1977; Brown, 1985; Jones, 1993).

Modes of adaptation

Berry (1992; 1994; 1997) has proposed a model which helps us to explore the adaptation style of the Asian immigrants in Britain and elsewhere. The model is embedded in social psychology and has been successfully applied to study the immigrants' predicament in a variety of cultural contexts. Berry (1994) defines acculturation as 'a culture change that results from continuous, first hand contact between two distinct cultural groups.' He suggests four acculturation strategies employed by immigrants as they seek an answer to two major issues, namely, is it considered to be of value to maintain cultural identity? And, is it considered to be of value to maintain relationships with other groups? The responses of minority groups to these two questions range from positive/positive (integration), positive/negative (separation), negative/positive (assimilation) to negative/negative (marginalization).

The major shortcoming of the model (not a theory as he claims; see Berry (1997)) is that it underplays the significance of the attitudes, values and the *zeitgeist* of the receiving society. Canada is a good example to illustrate this point. Although Canadian society has an open multicultural policy compared with Britain, people of Afro-Caribbean and Indian origin and other people of colour still face more discrimination than do white immigrants (Fisher and Echols, 1989). This is largely due to the residual colonial attitude of white superiority towards people of the third world. The decision to integrate or not to integrate does not entirely rest on the immigrants and their descendants but also – perhaps more so – on the reaction of the host society. If the institutions of the judiciary, the police, the civil service and employers are prejudiced, there is little incentive for the offspring of the immigrants to integrate. A conceptual weakness of Berry's model is that it unduly emphasizes the immigrants' (and their offspring's) response to the acculturation process. There are other very cogent objections, both conceptual and procedural, raised by fellow scholars in the field (see Kagitcibasi, 1997; Horenczyk, 1997; Lazarus, 1997). Despite these shortcomings, the model has given direction to a host of empirical studies and has provided a coherent structure within this growing field of interest.

Although no empirical research using this mode has been conducted in the UK to chart the adaptation strategies of the Asian groups in

Britain, it is quite instructive to do so with the aid of previous work in the field. From the accounts of researchers in this field (Dhaya, 1972; Anwar, 1978; Shaw, 1988; Singh, 1988; Desai, 1963; Watson, 1975), it may be inferred that the first generation immigrants had little more than a fleeting contact – often only in their employment – with the indigenous whites. This was due mainly to their lack of English language skills and their unfamiliarity with social mores on the one hand, and to their distinctive religious and social practices and their rural background on the other. Added to this is the fact noted earlier in this chapter that they were discriminated against in housing and employment and, generally, were given a hostile reception.

Although Asian immigrants enjoyed all civic rights in the UK, including voting, their *de facto* position was one of social, and in some cases geographical, separation from the white British. Rose *et al.* (1969) described the situation of Muslims in their authoritative report:

Pakistanis in Britain regard themselves as a people apart. They classify themselves as Kale *(Black), and European as* Gore lok *(literally 'white people') . . . The terms are continually used by the Pakistani imimmigrants, whether they are peasants or members of the educated elite, and they serve to heighten the consciousness of racial, social, and cultural differences.*
(Rose and Deakin, 1969, p. 448)

Watson (1977), who carried out an in-depth study of immigrant Chinese communities in Hong Kong and Britain, writes 'that the economic niche (take-away and restaurants) that the Chinese control allows the immigrant to live and work, and prosper without changing their way of life to suit British expectations'. His conclusions concur with the findings of the previous researchers in the field in that the Chinese are by far the least integrated of all Britain's immigrant minorities: the development of Chinatowns in British cities and in North America is in some way a testimony to this situation. It is important to state a caveat here: by no means *all* Chinese immigrants in Britain (and elsewhere for that matter) are involved in the catering business; there is a minority of educated professionals who have isolated themselves from their 'countrymen' and who live in suburbia and are integrated with the indigenous whites.

From an analysis of the previous literature, it becomes apparent that by and large the first generation Asians employed 'separation' as a mode of working and living in Britain.

Identities of the first generation

A major part of this book is concerned with the identities of the offspring of the first generation Asian immigrants. Therefore, it is important to discuss briefly how the personal and social identities of the Asian immigrants have been influenced and shaped by their ethnic and religious affiliations. Newly arrived immigrants all over the world tend to retain and even reinforce their existing identities to cope with their sense of the loss of 'home ethos'. Asians had a total commitment to their religion and culture, but with the passage of time they begin to shift their longing for the 'home' in Pakistan and India to a greater identification with Britain as was noted by the psychologically-focused research of Stopes-Roe and Cochrane (1990). They found that 59 per cent of first generation parents think Britain is their home country now while only four per cent are uncertain. The authors observe: 'The passage of time, however, had changed many parents, so that Britain "feels like my own country because I've been here so long". For some parents more years had been spent in Britain than in the country of origin: "I have spent more time here now, in fact I have become old in this country" said one; to another Britain "was home, since I have lived here for 40 years but only 14 years there".' However, when it came to the question of *personal identity*, only one person, out of a sample of 120, opted for British identity, and the rest described themselves as Indian/Pakistani. The authors argue that this is quite consistent with the stance that Britain is home for the majority but that 'the customs and culture of the natives and their attitudes towards himself and his people may preclude a personal feeling of being one of them'. However, it is interesting to note that 74 per cent of the young people in the study regarded Britain as their home country and 56.7 per cent thought their identity to be British – a remarkable difference from the first generation. I will develop the argument further in *Chapter 4*.

Socialization of the younger generation

The first generation Asian parents, in general, brought up their children and trained their young people as they themselves were brought up in their country of origin. Whilst detailed discussion of this topic is beyond the scope of this book, it is important to give a brief sketch of the socialization practices (for details, see Dosanjh and Ghuman, 1996). The upbringing of children in traditional families tends to follow a similar pattern; hence, I will discuss the general patterns for the Asian groups and mention exceptions to the rules where relevant.

Children are brought up to be obedient and respectful of their elders in the family and community around them. Through a variety of implicit and explicit methods and interactions, children are taught to be inter-dependent and not 'individualistic' and independent. Social conformity is demanded of the offspring and any sign of individuality is seen as a threat to the authority of the head of the family who, invariably, is the father.

South Asians are more prone to show affection and love for their children, whereas Chinese parents, according to Sung (1967), think they can maintain their authority if they are careful to maintain a certain distance from their children. Religious training is considered by parents to be very important for the cultivation of filial piety and humility. Assertiveness and self-pride are considered to be negative attributes in a child and young person, and are discouraged. Drawing from her own personal experiences, Sung (*Ibid.*, p.172) writes on the training of Chinese children: 'He is taught that forbearance, patience, and self-sacrifice are virtues and that self-interest must be subordinated to the larger good, whereas the American child is encouraged to give free expression to his personality in a very permissive atmosphere'.

Young people are expected to be loyal to the family, to be obedient to their parents and to give due respect to their elders. The choice of education of young people is to be left in the hands of their parents who are considered to know best the interests of the child and his/her future. Likewise, the choice of marriage partner is thought best left to the parents or 'match makers' and go-betweens. Dating and courting were virtually unknown among the first generation immigrants and they have taught their children the perceived drawbacks of love-marriages and the dangers of pre-marital and promiscuous sex.

The second generation parents have changed their socializing practices in that the salience of religion has lessened, as have the elaborate rituals surrounding pregnancy and childbirth (Dosanjh and Ghuman, 1996). Furthermore, large families (those having more than three children) have given way more often to the British norm of the two child nuclear family in which the parents are more prone to give freedom to their children to pursue their interests and hobbies and they are more likely to treat their girls on a par with boys, particularly in access to education. There has been a shift in the languages spoken at home; most of the second generation families are bilingual and their British-born children increasingly use English as their first language. The second generation families are materially better off, partly because of the rise in general prosperity in Britain but, more importantly, because mothers are increasingly going out to work – thus also gaining independence and personal autonomy from their husbands.

There is no research known to the writer on the Chinese in Britain, but research by Li-Repac (1982) in the US found that, with acculturation, the second generation Chinese, predictably, are nearer to the American norms in rearing their children, namely, allowing them more independence and autonomy, having smaller families and fathers sharing the childcare chores with mothers.

Summary

To understand fully the predicament of Asian young people in Western societies, it is important to know the historical and socio-cultural factors which have transpired to bring about the current situation. The first generation immigrants brought with them religions, cultural values and social mores which are fundamentally different from those of indigenous people in the UK. In the case of the Chinese, with the exception of a few professionals, most people found jobs in restaurants and continued their traditional style of life with little contact with the indigenous whites. The people from the Indian sub-continent, on the other hand, had a broader employment profile but most of them were still mainly concentrated in heavy industry, and the majority of the educated ones (see Fryer, 1984) were forced to find their niche in bus-conducting.

The most telling problem for the first generation Asians was their inability to speak and write English. Those who had knowledge of English still found it difficult to communicate because of the differences in pronunciation and diction. This handicap proved to be a major hurdle in finding suitable employment, and for general communication with the indigenous British. Equally, the residual post-colonial attitude of superiority held by the white British further alienated the newcomers. The vast majority settled in inner-city areas and rebuilt their social and religious institutions which helped them to develop their own distinctive life styles. These enclaves served the twin role of providing social and cultural continuity with their home traditions together with physical and psychological security.

In the 1960s (and even in the early 1970s), the immigrants made few special demands on education, health and other social services. They acquiesced in what was offered them, which was often second-class (see Rex and Tomlinson, 1979), in jobs, housing and other civic amenities. This was primarily due to two reasons: that the majority (in particular the Chinese) felt that they were going to be in this

country for a short period only, that is, as sojourners, and the fact
that they were voluntary immigrants and doing well materially
compared with their situation back home.

The offspring of immigrants are beginning to move towards
integration and assimilation through inter-marriage, some staying
at the 'separation' mode and a few becoming marginalized (alienated)
as they reject both the norms of the family and those of wider British
society. In the next chapter I will discuss in detail the predicament
of those of the second and third generations – the majority of whom
are UK-born and British citizens (Anwar, 1998).

Further reading

Helweg, W. A. and Helweg, M. U. (1990). *An Immigrant Success Story:
East Indians in America*. London: Hurst & Company.
A readable account of immigrants from India (mainly Hindus and Sikhs)
to America and should provide a useful perspective in understanding the
situation of Indians in Britain.

de Lepervanche, M. M. (1984). *Indians in a White Australia: An account
of race, class and Indian immigration to eastern Australia*. London: Allen
& Unwin.
A general introduction to Indian migration to Australia and a detailed and
lucid anthropological study of a Punjabi community in a small town.

Rose, E. J. B. and Deakin, N. (1969). *Colour and Citizenship: A report
on British race relations*. Oxford: Oxford University Press for Institute
of Race Relations, London.
Part II is an excellent coverage of the first generations' socio-cultural
backgrounds as well as of the prevailing British socio-political climate of
the 1960s.

Shaw, A. (1988). *A Pakistani Community in Britain*. London: Basil
Blackwell.
Chapter 2 deals with the problems of the first generation and Chapter 8
takes up the issues relevant to the second generation.

Wong, Y-F. L. (1992). *Education of Chinese Children in Britain and the
USA*. Clevedon: Multilingual Matters.
Chapter 1 describes the Chinese communities in London, San Francisco and
New York City.

3

Adolescents of the Second and Third Generation

I feel as though I'm very Westernised, but then ... not completely, I'm not Chinese either. It's like I'm Chinese in blood, but I'm not Chinese mentally. I am more now than I used to be, but not how I'd like to be. I mean I would like to be bilingual in the true sense. .... It's not a culture conflict or clash, but there is some sort of conflict within me.
(Parker, 1995, p. 174)

All growing teenagers challenge to some extent the authority of their parents and assert their individuality in order to explore their own personal and social identities. For Asian youngsters, there are additional difficulties which arise because of the way in which the beliefs, values and social attitudes of their families often contrast with those of the host society. For this reason, their social and psychological development is likely to be more difficult than that of their white peers.

They have been referred to as the *Half-way Generation* (Taylor and Hegarty, 1985), the *In-Between Generation* (Taylor, 1976) and as having the *Best of Both Worlds* (Drury, 1991). Their primary socialization and subsequent nurturing has been largely based on traditional upbringing as described in the last chapter but their education at British schools exposes them to radically different values and beliefs in that the emphasis is on self-development, autonomy and gender equality.

A significant factor in their lives is that of racial prejudice and discrimination, as it was found to be with the first generation. As already mentioned, there is firm evidence to show that there is discrimination against Asians and blacks in all walks of life, including educational institutions, the Police, the Law and Civil Service (Modood *et al.* 1997; Jones, 1993). Anwar (1978; 1979; 1994) has carried out several studies on the prevalence of racial prejudice and discrimination in Britain. Summarizing his latest work, Anwar writes:

In my more recent research, I have discovered that, in areas like Birmingham, young Asians are very aware of the increasing number of racial harassment incidents and the extent of racial prejudice and discrimination, which are affecting race relations. However, on the whole it appears that concerning racial attacks, relations with the police and race relations, young Asians are not very optimistic and more action needs to be taken ...
(Anwar, 1998, p. 97)

Racial prejudice is likely to undermine the self-esteem, personal identity and general confidence of Asian young people and is also a major barrier to integration into the mainstream British way of life. Therefore, a major part of this chapter is devoted to a discussion of the extent of racial discrimination and its psychological explanation. I will also look at gender equality of the West versus role differentiation of Asians; individuality and self-expression versus collectivity and emphasis on family values; and secular outlook versus religious orientation.

Racial discrimination and prejudice

The first generation tacitly accepted the racial discrimination meted out to them as many thought that it was the price they had to pay for their voluntary migration. However, their progeny are less likely to accept this disadvantage, and are prone to demand its redress. The riots of Brixton, Toxteth and Handsworth (England) in the 1980s (and, more recently, riots in Bradford by Muslim youths – see *The Observer*, 12 June, 1995) were in part due to the frustration of increasing unemployment and police harassment of ethnic minority youths.

Prejudice against ethnic minorities

The latest report of the Policy Studies Institute (Modood *et al.*, 1997) on the prejudice of white Britons against ethnic minorities paints a bleak picture. Over a quarter of the whites (women slightly less than men) in the sample admitted to being prejudiced against people from the Indian sub-continent, but less than one in ten reported being prejudiced against the Chinese – a significant difference to which I will return presently. In an in-depth study of adolescent boys and girls (white, Asian and black), Brannen *et al.* (1994) found that half of the white young people and parents in their study acknowledged that blacks and Asians have a harder time.

Table 3.1: Perceived prejudice against South Asians by whites in percentages (adapted from Roberts and Sachdev, 1996).

Degree of prejudice	Adults			Young People (age: 12–19)
	1987	1991	1994	1994
A lot	62	57	59	51
A little	30	35	34	41
Hardly any	6	4	5	4

A recent comprehensive survey (Roberts and Sachdev, 1996) of young people's opinions and perceptions of racial prejudice in Britain revealed a disturbing picture. A question asked in the survey was: 'Do you think there is a lot of prejudice against Asians in Britain nowadays, or a little, or hardly any?'. *Table 3.1*, adapted from the study, shows the responses.

Amongst the other salient findings of the survey was that a significantly higher percentage of girls think there is prejudice than do boys; this is also the case with the older age group (18- to 19-year-olds). On the question of their own prejudice (self-rated), it was found that nearly a quarter of young people claimed they were only 'a little' prejudiced compared with around a third of the adults in 1994, which is a slight increase in reported prejudice levels by adults since 1991. The authors did not wish to draw the obvious conclusion that younger people are less prejudiced than adults as the explanation might be more to do with 'trying to please the interviewer', also known in the literature as the *desirability response set* (see Oppenheim, 1966). However, a reassuring finding was that nearly 82 per cent of the boys and girls said they would not mind a relative marrying an 'Asian'. Likewise, the majority of the Asian young people (67 per cent) said they would not mind if a close relative were to marry a white person.

Discrimination in employment

To conclude the summary of this comprehensive survey, let us turn now to perceived discrimination in employment. To the question 'On the whole do you think people of Asian origin are not given jobs these days because of their race . . . a lot, a little, or hardly at all?', 17 per cent thought there was 'a lot' of discrimination whereas 50 per cent thought there was 'a little' and 28 per cent thought there was 'hardly any at all'. The figures given for the adults are somewhat higher than these, but not significantly for the prejudiced categories

(23 and 42 per cent respectively). The survey also reveals that white young people perceive the judicial system to be biased against Asians and blacks.

In a large-scale survey of opinion of young people in the mid-1980s, Furnham and Gunter (1989) also found a prevalence of racial prejudice among white young people but they end on an optimistic note. There was evidence of racial prejudice and discrimination; indeed, over a third admitted that they were a 'little' prejudiced, but the vast majority who expressed opinions believed in equality between 'races', the use of anti-discriminatory legislation, and close integration between groups.

The recent report of the PSI (Modood *et al.*, 1997) summarizes the results of their survey as follows and confirms the results of Roberts and Sachdev (1996) with the younger generation:

The point here is that there is now a consensus across all groups that prejudice against Asians [South Asians] *is much the highest of any ethnic, racial or religious groups; and it is believed by Asian people themselves that the prejudice against Asians is primarily a prejudice against Muslims.*
(Modood *et al.*, 1997, p. 133, my parentheses)

There is a substantial body of empirical research (Brown, 1985; Jones, 1993) which links racial discrimination in employment, housing and other walks of life to racial prejudice against Asians – although some groups, such as Chinese and Indians, have fared better in a recent survey (Modood *et al.*, 1997). An experimental study conducted by two doctors (Esmail and Everington, 1997) highlights the extent of discrimination against South Asians by the National Health Service of England and Wales. They constructed a matched sample (age, sex, qualifications, experience and general interests) of fifty applicants for work in general hospital employment where the name of the applicant was the only major distinguishing feature in their curriculum vitae. It was found that only 36 per cent of the applicants with Asian names were short listed, compared with 52 per cent of those with English names. This investigation is a replication of the research conducted by the authors in 1991 when they found a similar pattern of discrimination (Esmail and Everington, 1993). To conceal their ethnic origin there is a tendency (Ghuman, 1994; 1995b; Helweg and Helweg, 1990) amongst Asian young people to anglicize their names to avoid such 'first level discrimination', that is, where applications are rejected on the basis of name only. The present author (Ghuman,1994) has interviewed young Sikh boys and girls who have omitted the obligatory middle names of *Singh* and *Kaur* respectively and shortened their first names to sound more like English ones.

Thus, Surrinder becomes 'Sue', and Daljit becomes 'David' and Harminder 'Harry' and so on. Helweg and Helweg (1990) found a similar trend among the people of Indian subcontinent origin in the USA. Likewise, most young people of Chinese origin in Britain are prone to use a Christian name which is Anglo-Saxon (Wong, 1987). Tajfel (1992) notes the strategy of changing names among Jewish people in England. He writes of '. . . where changing one's name does not present much difficulty and can often get one off the hook of being foreign born or of foreign descent. There was a time in England when a physician called Goldsmith could get more easily his first job in a hospital than one called Goldschmidt' (p. 15).

The extensive PSI research survey by Moodod *et al.* (1997) already noted reveals the extent of discrimination faced by the second generation. For instance, the rate of unemployment amongst people under 35 years of age of Pakistani and Bangladeshi origin is 'much higher than white and Indian/African Asian men' of similar educational qualifications. The authors conclude their section on employment with these words:

. . . that most, but not all, the groups are still disadvantaged, but not evenly so. There is in fact only one circumstance in which all the minorities are disadvantaged: they are all substantially under-represented in the most elite jobs, namely as employers and managers in large establishments. This could be said to be a 'glass ceiling' that affects all non-white men equally.
(Moodod *et al.*, 1997, p. 143)

This 'glass ceiling' effect may be due to a combination and interplay of many factors but it is highly likely that racial prejudice is implicated in the explanation. This is the common perception of whites as well as of the non-whites sampled in the research.

In order to understand the racism encountered by Asians and other minority groups we have to turn to social psychological theories and other relevant literature in the field.

Nature of racial prejudice

Allport (1954) seems to favour an individualistic interpretation but does not underestimate the influence of in-groups and social structures:

This volume maintains that prejudice is ultimately a problem of personality formation and development; no two cases of prejudice

are precisely the same . . . But it likewise maintains that one of the frequent sources, perhaps the most frequent source, of prejudice lies in the needs and habits that reflect the influence of in-group memberships upon the development of the individual personality.
(p. 41)

But, later in his book, he is more emphatic on the social context of prejudice: 'Prejudice is a social fact, and it seems to require a social context' (p. 344).

The psychoanalytical school of psychology, on the other hand, seeks the explanation of racial prejudice (as of most other human behaviour) in the unconscious mind and in the early parent–child interaction. Prejudice, according to these theorists (see Webster, 1995), covers up for severe inferiority feelings; or gives security; or is bound up with repressed sexuality; or helps to relieve guilt feelings. Such an analysis goes on to suggest that as the motives for prejudice spring from the subconscious mind, few people know the real reason(s) for their hatred of minority groups. The reasons they invent are merely rationalizations (Allport, 1954).

Another well-researched psychological theory, which explains behaviour at an individual level, is that of Adorno (see Adorno *et al.*, 1950). He argues that the prejudiced personality tends to be ethnocentric, that is, it idealizes the group it belongs to and shows hostility to outgroups. The cluster of personality traits which are found in ethnocentric people are those of authoritarianism (need for submission to strict authority) and moral rigidity, especially on sexual matters, where deviation from the norms should be severely disapproved of and punished. Such individuals tend to attribute undesirable character traits (such as being lazy, dishonest, exploitative) to outgroups, using the projection mechanism described above. Furthermore, Adorno and colleagues (see Adorno *et al.*, 1950) argue that the genesis of the authoritarian personality is to be found in early upbringing: parents of such a type of personality tend to be harsh and too demanding and are zealously interested in their own social status. This theory is supposed to be a universal one, in that it is applicable to all groups and held to be valid for explaining the behaviour of prejudiced personalities. However, Aboud (1988), summarizing the research findings on this theory, concludes 'the basic proposition of this theory is that authoritarian child-rearing practices of parents determine prejudice in children. There is no evidence for such a relation in the research reported here, except in adolescent boys'.

Development of racial prejudice

Children enter a social world in which ethnic, gender, social class and other distinctions are generally made and in which language labels and associated stereotypes exist for their description. According to the research findings of Davey (1983), children acquire ethnic distinctions quite early on in their lives: 'by the age of seven or eight they have not only learned the standard classification system but also what attitudes should be adopted to people classified in a particular way'. Children learn to use the category system (labels) quite unwittingly. 'Children learn to describe them in favourable or unfavourable terms. They acquire the linguistic tags which are applied to them and the behaviour it is appropriate to adopt towards them,' argues Davey (1983, p. 56). In other words, children develop a schema, or cognitive framework, to deal with the information connected with their own race and other race children. Milner (1983) puts it succinctly:

But selective processes may operate to absorb only information that is congruent, so that the establishment of this first, basic evaluative foundation is extremely influential in determining the course of later attitude development.
(Milner, 1983, p. 110)

The development of ethnic awareness and prejudices in children has been discussed among others by Goodman (1964), Katz (1976) and Aboud (1988).

Goodman proposes three stages in the development of children's attitudes towards race, namely: racial awareness, racial orientation and, finally, racial attitudes. I will discuss in some detail the cognitively-formulated theory of Aboud (1988, 1993), which takes into account the salient points of Katz's model and also that of Goodman.

Aboud's theory of the development of ethnic awareness and prejudices

Aboud (1993) proposes a model which is based explicitly on Piaget's model of conceptual and moral development. She argues that children's development of ethnic awareness, preferences and the 'nature of prejudices' closely corresponds to the Piagetian stages of cognitive development. The pre-operational child (aged two to seven), who is perceptually orientated and finds difficulties in doing conservation tasks (of mass, weight and number), tends to show more prejudice against children of other races than do older children.

39

Children's judgements at this stage are partial and fragmentary in that they do not inter-relate given information in problem-solving situations. Around the age of seven onwards – the beginning of the concrete stage of thinking – racial prejudice in children declines as they become mature thinkers. They develop the ability to differentiate between a real change in substance as opposed to changes in appearance and then become more logical in making judgements on such tasks as class inclusion. For instance, children at this level of maturity begin to appreciate that blacks and whites can be both good and bad, unlike the premature thinking of the younger child who is prone to see things as merely 'black' and 'white'! Aboud (1988) concludes:

In summary, there is evidence that the way children interpret ethnic differences and ethnic affiliation stems in part from their understanding of other physical and social phenomenon. Ethnic cognitions appear to develop as a function of the child's general cognitive development'.
(p. 103)

The second Piagetian notion which Aboud (1993) finds useful in her model is that of *egocentrism*. This concept is generally defined as children's inability to see things from other than their own perspective. In speech, for instance, they do not attempt to see themselves from the point of view of their hearer (Donaldson, 1978). This failure to accept a different perspective on things can also extend to ways of dressing, eating and general behaviour. Consequently, young children (aged five to eight) tend to deduce and make value judgements that other people's ways of doing things are necessarily wrong. Aboud (1988) argues from her empirical studies that, around the age of nine plus, children develop the mental maturity to differentiate between their attitudes towards other ethnic groups and their own knowledge (cognition) of them. Her illustrative example is: 'I do not like this person but I can see that he has some good qualities that another might like or I like this person but I can see that he is not all good'. In ethnic attitude formation, Aboud argues that the basic processes proceed from the affective (like and dislike) to the perceptual (colour and other visible factors) and finally to the cognitive. The saliency in the early stages (ages three to five) is that of affect, which later gives way to perceptual orientation (ages five to seven) and finally to the cognitive orientation which is achieved at age seven plus. The second sequence, according to Aboud, relates to a change in the focus of attention, from self to group through to individual focus. These two sequences overlap and explain the development of racial attitude in children within a given social context.

Shortcomings of the model

This closely argued model, which cites many empirical researches in support of its validity, has its shortcomings. Firstly, it is arguable whether the affective factor can be disassociated from the cognitive: feeling and thinking about things often go together. There is empirical support for this from the study of Tajfel *et al.* (1972), who found that children's *feelings* about countries, for example, good, poor, I like, emerged before the *facts* about the countries. The Piagetian model is a 'rational model' of intellectual development in that cognition plays an important role and feelings come later. Therefore, its application to explain the development of prejudice by Aboud overstates the role of cognition.

Another shortcoming is that the Piagetian theory of development underrates the developing abilities of children and excessively relies on formal logic rather than on the language and motivation of the children and the context in which children are given problems to solve (Bruner, 1971; Donaldson, 1978).

Milner's theory

In contrast to Aboud, Milner (1983) underlines the importance of the socialization process in the transmission of racial prejudice. He argues that, when racial prejudice has been incorporated into the mainstream culture and its institutions, it is not the individual we should turn to for the explanation of prejudice but to the social environment and the socialization processes themselves. He writes: 'Children are apparently sensitive to the most subtle nuances of social influences and incorporate them in their nascent attitudes' (p. 73). Furthermore, he suggests that children's racial attitudes and behaviour often show close similarity to those of their parents.

Milner's (1983) studies of adolescence report relatively little change in the children's attitudes towards various ethnic and national groups as they approach their teenage years and late adolescence. Indeed, he argues that the racial attitudes tend towards greater consistency and stability as adolescents approach adulthood.

To be sure, there are going to be individual differences in the way children and young people express their feelings, thinking and behaviour concerning race, due to their different personalities and social situations. However, children construct their categories and make their comparisons within a framework of values and social mores which is not of their own creation (Davey, 1983, p. 178). Labels and stereotypes about Asians and other ethnic minorities are widely used in Britain and elsewhere and we must now briefly turn our attention to these notions.

Racial stereotypes

Allport (1954) defines a stereotype as 'Whether favourable or unfavourable a stereotype is an exaggerated belief associated with a category. Its function is to justify (rationalise) our conduct in relation to that category' (p. 191). Allport argues that stereotypes should not be confused with 'categories', which are there to describe our social world, but rather should be understood as devices for categorical acceptance or rejection of a group. The contemporary interpretation of stereotypes is, however, somewhat equivocal (Leyens *et al.*, 1994; Davey, 1983) in that they are thought to serve the same functional need as categories, namely to filter and thus to simplify our perception and thinking concerning the social world.

The growing child learns the stereotypical images of its own group and that of other ethnic groups from his/her family and in the local neighbourhood. These are sometimes reinforced by the media, but there is no firm evidence to support this contention (see Durkin, 1992). Adolescents tend to maintain these stereotypes by using a rule of 'exception' or 'atypical' to handle negative exemplars which do not fit their preconceptions. Gaine (1988) collected a sample of writing from 13-year-old boys and girls on racism. The response of an Asian girl is revealing of how the rule of exception is used by young white people to maintain their *Paki* stereotypes of Asians:

I resent the fact of being called a Paki in as much as I wouldn't call someone fatty or skinny, or four eyes. Paki to me is an insult as much as 'curry muncher' is, what if I didn't like curry?. . . What I don't understand is when people say to me ' Oh, you're okay, because you're very westernised, it's just the rest'. Well I do happen to be a very big part of the rest. This is very insulting. (Gaine, 1988, p. 12)

The word *Paki* has been used by adolescents to describe all Asians (except Chinese) in schools (Kelly, 1990), and this has stereotyped meanings implying: small shopkeepers, people who wear outlandish clothes, who coerce their daughters into arranged marriages, and who are dirty and money-grabbing. Allport (1954) concluded the findings from his survey of researches that ethnic minorities in the US used the same disparaging labels as did the whites to describe other minority groups. Sherif and Sherif (1969) also note that minority groups use negative stereotypes similar to the ones used by the dominant group when describing other groups. This explains the fact that adolescents of West Indian ancestry call their Asian counterparts *Pakis* and that the latter reciprocate by using the names *nigger* and *sambo* (see Kelly, 1990).

In-groups and out-groups

It was noted earlier in this chapter that the explanation of prejudice in terms of the individual's anxieties, conflicts and motivations does not adequately explain inter-group prejudices and discrimination. Groups are not merely collections of individuals but develop their own norms, goals and values which override individual dispositions and provide motivation for action. Tajfel (1973) stresses the importance of understanding group dynamics in order to explain the behaviour of individuals.

The need to understand the dynamic nature of in-groups versus out-groups and the ways in which this influences individuals is paramount. Sherif and Sherif (1969) undertook pioneering studies of adolescents which are still considered to be a landmark in the history of social psychology. These studies were planned to discover the effect of group membership (that is, in-group) on the behaviour of its individual members. For the details of the studies, the reader is referred to the original reports, but the main findings can be summarized as follows. Firstly, even arbitrarily-formed groups over a short period developed their own norms, hierarchy and rudimentary culture. Secondly, under conditions of competition, inter-group hostilities grew, negative stereotypes of out-group members began to emerge while in-group solidarity intensified. Thirdly, when the boys in the study had to co-operate to accomplish goals, which were in the interest of both groups, the tension and hostility lessened and relative harmony prevailed. Duckitt (1992) argues that social categorization acts by triggering a basic motivational process: a need to evaluate one's group positively relative to out-groups.

An example from the Sherifs' (1969) research should be instructive. The two groups studied by them were named the *Red Devils* and the *Bull Dogs*. The authors described their behaviour in competitive sports:

In 1949, the Red Devils began to slip behind in the competition, thereupon accusing the Bull Dogs of being 'dirty players' and 'cheats' ('At least we play fair'). The victorious Bull Dogs were elated, happy, self-content, and full of pride. The losing Red Devils were dejected. . . . Particularly common was the term 'pigs'. Among the names used by most Bull Dogs for Red Devils on this and other occasions were 'pigs', 'dirty bums' or 'Red bums', 'jerks', and several more objectionable terms.
(Sherif and Sherif, 1969, p. 242)

Now witness a typical comment by a white student, when his teacher asked him to write about Asians:

Michael: *I think the black people should live in society where they won't be talked about as not a human species. Even though I call blacks names they can take the mouth. They take over most of the shops and usually they smell of some sort . . . they don't go around calling us names. Pakistanis are taking over the population.*
(Gaine, 1988, p, 8)

Billig and Tajfel (1973) found that two groups arbitrarily set up for experimental work behaved in a discriminatory way towards one another: 'It seems the mere mention of 'groups' by the experimenters was sufficient to produce strong intergroup discrimination' (p. 48). The experimental work of Tajfel and his co-workers (Tajfel, 1978) has shed much light on inter-group conflict and rivalry.

Tajfel's Social Identity Theory

Tajfel's *Social Identity Theory* is formulated from extensive empirical research with social groups. Simply put, it states that there appears to be a need for every social group to create and maintain a positively-valued social identity, and that this is achieved by comparison to an out-group or groups who are often characterized negatively. The membership of a group may be based on the criteria of social class, caste, race (physical features), ethnicity (culture), religion, language or, indeed, on any other identifiable and consensually arrived at measure.

At a school level, the following anecdotal example illustrates out-group hostility in that a mere mention of Asians provokes in some young white people the most insulting and racist remarks. A former student of the University of Wales, who teaches in a mainly 'South Asian' secondary school in Birmingham, UK, described with some puzzlement his younger brother's reaction to the Asian communities:

I am amazed and shocked what my younger brother says about Asians when I talk about my school. He is a nice kid – you know with usual problems of growing up – but the sort of things he says about Asians makes me cringe with despair. Pakis are dirty, they bring disease into this country, they are taking over our jobs, they smell and are dirty. And the funny thing is he hasn't met any Muslim or black kids in his life. He tells me most of his mates say things like that and have been out Paki-bashing.

At a societal level the power relations between groups is one of the important determining factors in explaining discriminatory behaviour in employment, housing and education. For instance, the hegemony of *brahmins* and other high-castes in India had denied the untouchables (Harijan – an out-group) their civic, economic and political rights for over a millennium. Their plight is only marginally better despite the affirmative actions of the last fifty years.

To conclude this section, it is apposite to present the arguments of Duckitt (1992) on racial prejudice. He argues that psychological factors operate to modulate the impact of social influences upon the individual's thinking and behaviour. Therefore, explanations of racial prejudice which are based on personality factors only are going to be inadequate. In order to fully understand the nature of prejudice, he suggests, not only do we have to study the individual as a member of several social groups but also place our discussion within wider historical and socio-political contexts and pay attention to the 'situational factors'.

Gender inequalities

How far do the specific gender roles and behaviour, which the first generation practised prior to migration, persist in today's younger generation? There is research evidence (Ghuman, 1994; Drury, 1991) to suggest that, although the gross forms of inequalities between girls and boys have attenuated, the former are still not treated by parents on a par with the latter. Girls are given less personal freedom and choice than boys in the selection of friends, clothes, seeking jobs away from home and in going out with their friends. Ghuman's (1994) investigation of young Asian people found that over three-quarters of the sample thought that girls were not treated the same, although Hindu and Sikh parents are more liberal than the Muslims. The young people's comments are illuminating of the parents' attitudes. A fourteen-year-old Muslim girl showed her strong feelings:

My brother plays till 8– he is allowed out. I go home, do my homework, watch TV and sleep. It is like a rota. Next day is exactly the same – weekends are the same.
(Ghuman, 1994, p. 60)

The author's research also encompassed fieldwork on South Asian young people in Canada, where he found evidence to support the view that Hindu and Sikh parents are increasingly giving more educational opportunities to their daughters, but still are more protective in the social sphere. Other researchers have found a similar trend. Drury (1991) carried out her fieldwork in Nottingham with 102 Sikh young girls (16- to 20-years-old) and found that a majority of them were resentful of the unequal treatment given to boys. A Sikh girl gave vent to her feelings:

I would like to have a boyfriend and I would like to have a love marriage but the consequences are too great. Gossip spreads and you can lose everything. Everyone in the family can be hurt and nobody will want to marry my sister . . . I think that Sikh boys in England are given too much freedom. They can go out with white girls yet they expect to marry an innocent Indian girl.
(Drury, 1991, p. 396)

Dating and relationships

The question of dating and pre-marital sex is an extremely difficult one for Asian young people. For white and African-Caribbean adolescents, it is an important part of the rites of passage to adulthood and to attaining independence. A quote from Moore and Rosenthal's book (1993) on adolescent sexuality illustrates this point:

Sexual behaviour is one of the key ways, in modern society, for adolescents to 'de-satellite' or begin, emotionally, to leave the family orbit and move towards independence. Successful moves towards gradual attainment of adult sexuality will heighten feelings of self-esteem and perceived competence to cope.
(Moore and Rosenthal, 1993, p. 37)

Asian communities in Britain and elsewhere strongly disapprove of dating, although they are prone to turn a blind eye if it is their sons who are 'going out' with white girls. Their hope is that boys will grow out of such transient relationships and eventually return to the fold and marry within their own community (see Wilson, 1978; Ballard, 1994). This fundamental difference on personal relation-ships, between home and the host society, is one of the major points of inter-generational conflict and tension in Asian families, especially with young girls.

Drury (1991) found that one fifth of the girls in her sample were secretly dating boys and some were going to pubs and drinking without the knowledge or consent of their parents. Likewise, the author (Ghuman, 1994) learnt from teachers in the Midlands and London areas of the UK that a significant number of boys and girls are covertly dating and this has caused a great deal of pain and anguish among parents. In a university town in Canada, Vaidyanatthan and Naidoo (1989) found that the majority (80 per cent) of second generation Indian young people from upper-middle class backgrounds thought that dating was desirable, whereas only 68 per cent of their parents found dating acceptable and then only if the couple was committed to a permanent relationship. Thus, we see a vast difference in the opinion held by two generations even of educated middle-class Indians.

The burden of arranged marriages often falls on the women because of the patriarchal nature of the Asian family (Bhopal, 1997). In the traditional family set-up, it is the newly-married woman who moves into the house of her in-laws and who takes care of the extended family, although this custom has declined dramatically as newly-married couples are setting up their own homes. But it is still the bride who is supposed to adapt to the norms of the family she marries into. Bhopal writes:

Moslem women experience an intense form of private patriarchy, followed by Sikh and Hindu women. . . . There are significant changes occurring for the younger women in the sample, indicating a move away from private to public patriarchy.
(Bhopal, 1997, p. 148)

Compartmentalism

From the research findings it is clear that many South Asian and Chinese girls have to learn to cope with a double disadvantage: parental restriction on the one hand; and racial prejudice of the wider society on the other. Such a situation can lead to deep anxiety and a loss of self-confidence, which may result in identity diffusion. There is evidence in the literature (Drury, 1991; Shaw, 1988) which shows that girls employ a variety of psychological mechanisms to maintain the continuity, distinctiveness and self-esteem of their personal identities. Compartmentalization is an example of such a mechanism. Breakwell (1986, p. 95) describes its function: 'The capacity for compartmentalism is quite startling in some cases, where completely mutually self-definitions are held simultaneously'. On the one hand, South Asian girls learn to think and behave as obedient and respectful daughters wearing *salwar kameez* (tunic with baggy trousers) and speaking in Punjabi/Hindi at home. On the other, they wear European-style uniform and speak English at school and are engaging and assertive like their English peers. Some girls have even been known to cope with dating, which is anathema to most South Asian parents (see Drury, 1991). An example of this coping strategy is to be found in Ghuman (1995a), where an experienced Sikh teacher urged her Asian students to follow her example:

47

I say look I have grown up in this environment, I had to fight battles . . . Although I am very forthright, but I am very traditionalist at heart. I can fit into both cultures. In Indian society, I behave like an Indian, here in school I behave like an English. I am bicultural.
(Ghuman, 1995 p. 74)

Compromise change

Another mechanism which may be used in a situation of conflict is that of 'compromise change'. This strategy has also often been used by Asian girls and examples are to be found in Wilson's ethnographic research (1978). The following example is taken from Ghuman's (1994) research, for which teenage girls were interviewed in Vancouver:

I try to go Church, I try to fit in. I do my best – I still believe in my religion (Hindu), but I can fit in both religions. . . . (Pause) You have to; I do. I was raised here. My parents have tried to make me a Hindi [sic] – but I mix with East Indians and white people. Now my parents have accepted my biculturalism.
(Ghuman, 1994, p. 135)

Fundamental change

According to Breakwell (1986), a third psychological mechanism, namely, 'fundamental change', may be used by individuals to re-appraise their identity structure when other measures fail to reduce anxiety and conflict. Some Asian girls in Britain, for instance, have to give up any hope of a career and are obliged to accept arranged marriages because of parental pressure. They probably re-appraise their 'identity' and seek self-esteem and distinctiveness in being a good wife and a mother. In this situation, they usually sacrifice continuity of their ego-identity as it was expressed in their autonomy and personal choices prior to their marriage.

The 'marginal man'

To explain the situation of people caught up in the tussle between two distinctive cultural systems, Stonequist's (1937) theory of the 'marginal man' is of some interest. His notion of the 'marginal man/woman' suggests that threats to identity may lead to higher levels of deviance, excessive anxiety and psychiatric instability. The 'marginal man' is the person who straddles two cultures in society (for example, Asian young people in the West) or is being raised by two 'distinct' parental groups (such as children of ethnically mixed parentage). The marginal person may be rejected, and feel alienated, by one or both parents, by home or by school. According to Breakwell (1986), no conclusive empirical evidence has emerged to support this contention. However, Tizard and Phoenix's study (1993) found some support for the 'marginal' predicament of 'mixed-parentage' (African-Caribbean and white) young people. A fifth of their sample showed some of the 'marginal' characteristics: 'They wished that they were white, or that they were either black or white, rather than 'mixed' . . . We characterised this 20 per cent of the sample as having a problematic, rather than a negative racial identity . . .' (p. 161). However, the authors argue that, because of the radical social changes in British society (leading to more tolerance towards non-white Britons), people of mixed black and white parentage suffer less rejection than they did in the past. This is the only major published source available on mixed-race young people, and the author has not found any substantive research on Anglo-Indian or Anglo-Asian children and young people which he can refer to.

It is important to point out that there has been a sea-change in the attitudes and values of whites towards cultural diversity and 'mixed-parentage' children since the time when Stonequist argued his theoretical stance. Bi-culturalism and bilingualism are increasingly becoming the norm of US society (Phinney, 1996), and are also being recognized as part of British cultural diversity. Despite this, Stonequist's model still offers some insights into understanding the predicament of those South Asian girls and boys who find it difficult to resolve the 'culture conflict' of home and school.

Eating disorders

There is some evidence in the literature, although not conclusive by any means, to suggest that the 'chasm between home and school' may cause serious psychological tension and excessive anxiety, which in turn can lead to serious illnesses. A literature survey did reveal some studies (Ahmad *et al.*, 1994; Dolan, 1991; Lacy and Dolan, 1988) which had investigated the eating disorders of South Asian girls. According to Lacy and Dolan (1988), there had been no reported cases of bulimia or anorexia nervosa until those described in their own study. They identified one girl of Pakistani origin, three of mixed racial background and one of Jamaican origin as suffering from one or the other of the eating disorders. The authors claim that the actual referral of South Asian girls to the clinic was 'ten times less than their numbers in the catchment area population' would suggest. In her review of British-based studies, Dolan (1991, p. 74)) concluded: 'In most of these case reports clinical features and demographic data show no major differences from those reported in the white eating-disordered population, but some differences must be noted'. The differences pertain to clinical matters and to black anorectics and are not relevant to our discussion here. However, the author goes on to argue that many British studies have suggested 'cultural identity confusion' as a contributing etiological factor, but this cannot be disentangled from the wider encounter of two 'cultures': that of the patients, on the one hand, and that of the health professionals, on the other.

Bryant-Waugh and Lask (1991) reported clinical case studies of four South Asian girls (mean age 12.6 years), who were diagnosed as suffering from anorexia nervosa. The authors claimed (wrongly in my view) that these were the first reported studied in Asian youngsters and, subsequently, they have dealt with another four cases. They argued that the 'culture conflict' between home and school values did play a part in two of the cases, and concluded

The common tasks of adolescence, which include the formation of an integrated sense of self, the emergence of an independent self, and the acceptance of a sexual self, are undoubtedly problematic for many young people. It can be argued that issues of autonomy, control and sexuality may present particular difficulties for children and adolescents described in this paper.
(Bryant-Waugh and Lask, 1991, p. 232)

Suicide attempts

A small-scale study (Kingsbury, 1994) of South Asian and white adolescents who had taken overdoses throws some interesting insights into the predicaments of South Asian girls. All young people (aged 12–18) who attended the West Middlesex University Hospital, England, in an overdosed condition from February 1987 to April 1988 (and who were available for interview), were included in the study. Semi-structured interviews were conducted by child psychiatrists. The final sample on which the findings were based is not significantly different in age, sex ratio, ethnic distribution and suicide-intent rate from the participants not included in the study. In the South Asian sub-sample, the vast majority who took the overdose were girls, the ratio being: female, 12, to male, 1; as opposed to 3 to 1 for the whites. The researchers summarize: 'Although Asians were not found in the high suicidal intent group, the rates of depressive disorder, hopelessness, long premeditation time (greater than three hours) were all higher in Asian adolescents. . . . The social and parental relationships showed a picture of isolation in Asian adolescents' (p. 133). Asian young people (mostly girls) were more likely to say 'No' to such questions as: 'Do you meet with friends after school?'; 'Do you visit other friends' houses?'. They confided less in their parents and experienced more control by parents than did their white counterparts.

Merrill and Owens (1986) conducted a comparative study on self-poisoning by South Asians and whites in a hospital in Birmingham, UK. The authors summarize: 'The relative excess of marital problems in Asian females, compared with white females, could be seen as being due to those patients who blamed their marital problems on unwanted arranged marriages . . . Overt racial prejudice, although rife in the community, was implicated in only three Asian self-poisonings; this may have been due to under-reporting to a white psychiatrist'(p. 11–12). The researchers warn the reader about the validity of their findings as the information was given by the patients and was interpreted by the assessors who are white. However, these findings have been supported by Biswas (1990), who studied a sample of South Asian and white adolescents (aged 13–17) and found that the self-poisoning rate of Asian girls was higher than that of whites. Culture conflict is mentioned as a possible reason for self-poisoning by the South Asians, especially for girls. Glover *et al.* (1989) analysed the attendance records of patients (aged 10–24) with self-poisoning at a London hospital which serves an area with a large Bangladeshi population. They found no significant difference in the proportion of Asian females, compared with non-Asian, in the age groups of 10–14 and 20–25. However, Asian girls were significantly over-represented in the 15–19 age group. The authors attribute this high proportion to the conflict of Asian versus Western lifestyles which is aggravated during adolescence, thus to some degree reinforcing the trend found in other studies.

Although there have been no large-scale studies with controlled samples and conditions which demonstrate conclusively that South Asian girls are more prone to suffer from psychological ailments and psychiatric illness than either their white counterparts or South Asian boys, the findings of the research extant lead us to infer that there is some cause for concern. South Asian girls need counselling and other forms of support (more so than boys) to help them cope with their anxieties and personal worries during their adolescence. In *Chapter 6*, I will turn to this and other related issues.

Religious orientation

The pervasive influence of religion in the lives of Asian immigrants was discussed in some detail in the last chapter. We shall now look at to what extent the religious orientation of the immigrants has been passed on to their progeny.

The psychological function of religion (broadly interpreted as faith in God and providing a 'world view') cannot be underestimated. It provides security, a sense of 'belonging' and a distinctive identity for its adherents. Most Asian people have turned to their religion to seek succour during life crises (see Kakar, 1994).

Furnham and Stacey have argued for a positive role for religion:

It appears that young people attempt to integrate their developing concepts and ideas about death with their total world view and their life in this world. Comprehension of birth and growth, health and illness, ageing and physical decline, life and death, grief and mourning, the capacity of nations with nuclear weapons to destroy humanity comes gradually with experience and knowledge ... Religious beliefs provide a framework by which to understand death and many other moral issues.
(Furnham and Stacey, 1991, p. 112)

On the other hand, it is argued by the sceptics that it has a negative influence on the development of personality. Their position is well summarized once more by Furnham and Stacey (1991): 'It is clearly easy to introduce stereotypes, bigotry and hostility into religious upbringing and education, and sometimes this is done deliberately' (p. 131). Furthermore, excessive religious zeal has also been known to be a major cause of personal anxiety, guilt and mental psychosis.

The significance of religion to the younger generation can be inferred from *Table 3.2* which is adapted from a published large-scale survey of ethnic groups in the UK (Modood *et al.*, 1997). A sample consisting of two generations of Asians, African-Caribbeans and whites was questioned on the statement: 'Religion is very important to how I live my life'.

The attitude amongst the younger generation varies according to their religious affiliation. Those most in favour of religion are the Pakistani and Bangladeshi young people who value the importance of Islam in their lives. Indians and 'African-Asians' (Asians who

Table 3.2: Positive responses (in percentages) of ethnic groups on the importance of religion (adapted from Modood et al., 1997).

Age group	White	Caribbean	Indian	Asian from Africa	Pakistanis and Bangladeshis	Chinese
16–34	5	18	35	37	67	11
50+	20	57	59	64	82	31

immigrated from Africa), who are mostly Hindu and Sikhs, show an intermediate level of interest, whereas the Chinese show the least favourable attitude to religion. It is clear from the table that the decline of religion is very marked indeed between the two generations.

Drury's (1991) ethnographic research, discussed earlier in this chapter, with young Sikh girls (16- to 20-year-olds) in Nottingham, UK, found that 42 per cent went to the temple regularly and participated in worship and other ceremonies. However, she found that those who attended the Gurudwara found it difficult to follow the services and the reading from the *Granth Sahib* (Holy Book) as it was in *Gurbani* (old Punjabi). Forty-four per cent of Drury's (1991) sample said that they and their parents hardly ever attend the temples and might only go for weddings and festivals. She found that the important custom of keeping one's hair uncut on the body is only practised by a minority of young boys/men, although more girls have kept this practice. Likewise, other symbols of the religion have been modified to accommodate the imperatives of the British society.

Ghuman (1994) also found that, although over two thirds of the young people studied went to their places of worship, most of them had only a smattering of knowledge of their religion. This was largely attributed to the perceived lack of consideration for younger people at the places of worship. First generation priests, who are mostly in charge of Gurudwaras, temples and mosques, continue to conduct services in the orthodox vernacular (Punjabi/ Hindu) which is poorly understood by the younger generation as most of them prefer to express themselves in English.

Stopes-Roe and Cochrane (1990a) also dealt with religious matters in their research on Asian young people (18- to 21-year-olds). The responses are not given on a 'religious affiliation basis' but overall they found that over two thirds of young people thought the teaching of religion to be very important. The reasons given were mainly related to morality, spiritual development, identity formation and moral guidance. However, they found a decline in both the function and teaching of religion. The first generation viewed religion as largely serving a social function, whereas the younger people gave primacy to its spiritual and personal dimension. All of the first generation sample thought that the teaching of religion was very important, or important, whereas only 85 per cent of the young people gave these responses. There is also evidence of a change in practices amongst Hindu young people. Although Jackson and Nesbitt (1993) studied the religious development of a younger age group (8- to 12-year-olds), in my view their conclusions are also relevant to the older boys and girls:

For younger people, however, they no longer seem part of a total world view or way of life. For many, the satvik nature of food, for example, is a matter relevant to the performance of a ritual within the tradition and not to the whole way of life. It might be important for some of the children we studied to eat vegetarian food, but its precise type seems to be less important outside the ritual context, especially when socialising with non-Hindu Westerners . . . but they have [festivals] become 'special events', and, for the young at least, do not highlight an annual cycle of time that is part of a distinctly Hindu world view.
(Jackson and Nesbitt, 1993, p. 179)

In sum, the religious orientation and devotion of the younger generation in Britain and elsewhere has changed to a considerable degree. Religious rituals are being shed and young people are questioning the myths and superstitions surrounding their faiths. It may be argued (quite rightly) that a similar change of attitudes might have also taken place on the Indian sub-continent and Hong Kong and therefore the attitudinal change of the younger generation in the UK cannot be wholly attributed to the process of acculturation.

Chinese young people show even less interest in the subject than their South Asian counterparts. Even amongst the first generation Chinese there was not the same degree of religious zeal as found in the other Asian communities. This is supported by the fact that the Chinese communities have not recreated Buddhist temples and other places of worship in the UK on the same scale.

Summary

This chapter has dealt comprehensively with the topic of racial prejudice, gender issues and religious orientation among the second and third generations. Racial prejudice influences Asian young people's lives in a profound and all-pervasive way. There are multiple causes of, and explanations for, racial/ethnic prejudice. The discussion on personality variables of prejudice showed that these modulate the existing degree of prejudice prevalent in society and provide only part of the explanation. The group level explanation of prejudice, on the other hand, was found to be more fruitful and potent. The writings and research of Allport (1954), Sherif and Sherif (1969) and Billig and Tajfel (1973) point to the importance of understanding the dynamics of in-groups versus out-groups and the ways in which this influences individuals. Billig and Tajfel (1973), using concepts from their *Social Identity Theory*, show that there appears to be a

54

need for every social group to maintain a positively-valued social identity, and this is achieved by comparison to out-groups, who are often treated negatively.

Finally, Asian girls seem to be facing more difficulties and problems than boys because of the patriarchal set up of Asian families. However, the findings of research extant on their mental health are inconclusive.

Further reading

The Further reading for *Chapter 3* is combined with that for *Chapter 4*, and can be found on p. 81.

4
Ethnic Identity, Acculturation and Self-Image

Some of the questions which the growing adolescent begins to ask about him or herself are related to the quest for personal identity; such as, Who am I? What sort of person am I? Whom do I belong to? This search for personal identity is intermeshed with two other important identity explorations, namely, ethnicity and gender. How far an ethnic identity is central to personal identity is one of the questions which I shall pursue in this chapter. For instance, is ethnic identity a salient feature in young people's lives, or is it like other identities such as gender, social class and (later) occupation? If so, what possible effect does ethnic identity exercise on the personality, attitudes and behaviour of young people?

Acculturation of adult immigrants has been studied quite comprehensively by social psychologists (Berry, 1976; 1994; 1997; Furnham and Bochner, 1986) but research on adolescents is relatively scarce. For an in-depth understanding of Asian young people's psychological wellbeing and social adjustment, it is important to review these studies. In addition, critical examination of this process will help us to discover if there are any links with a family of other concepts, namely, *self-image*, *ego-identity*, *ethnic identity* and *bi-culturalism*. The latter part of the chapter is devoted to a discussion of these issues.

Identity development

Phinney (1990; 1992; 1996 a, b) argues that the development of ethnic identity follows a path similar to that of ego identity, as first postulated and described in some detail by Erikson (1968) in his seminal work.

Erikson theorized that there are eight psychosocial developmental stages which describe the whole life cycle. These eight stages represent a sequence of ego growth and have three components: physical, societal, and the development of psychological meaning for the individual as a result of the interaction of the first two elements. Identity within Erikson's framework is a developmental achievement. It is defined by Marcia (1994, p. 70) as 'a coherent sense of one's meaning to oneself and to others within a social context. This sense of identity suggests an individual's continuity with the past, a personally meaningful present, and a direction for the future'.

Erikson's fifth stage, 'Identity versus role confusion', relates to the period of adolescence. Although ego identity has its forerunners in previous stages of development, its crucial period of development is during middle to late adolescence. Kroger (1989) describes this phase as:

Drawing upon resolutions to earlier stages, one must now approach the task of identity formation. Erikson suggests fidelity is the essence of identity. To become faithful and committed to some ideological world view is the task of this stage; to find a cause worthy of one's vocational energies and reflecting one's basic values is the stuff to affirm and be affirmed by a social order that identity aspires.
(Kroger, 1989, p. 27)

It is during adolescence that there is a confluence of profound changes in body, mind and sexuality. In body, young people are rapidly gaining height and weight and changes in voice due to glandular development. They are approaching a physical maturity which is close to that of adults. Intellectually, they progress from the concrete stage to the formal stage of thinking (Piaget, 1952; 1959). The characteristics of a 'formal' thinker are that he or she can *explain* physical and social issues rather than just *describe* them; he or she goes beyond the information given and can formulate hypotheses and is capable of testing these systematically. He or she makes mature judgements in that more than one alternative explanation is considered and accepted or rejected in the light of evidence[i]. Young people are more questioning, and even challenging, of established ways of doing things. Questions such as the following may be posed: Why is there homelessness in an affluent society? What is the point of having nuclear armaments, if the threat from the former Soviet Union isn't there any more? Why can't marijuana and Ecstasy be made legal and widely available?

The profound sexual changes have a marked effect on the emotional and social life of adolescents. Mood swings are known to be common amongst teenagers as are their capricious likes and dislikes of the opposite sex. All these dramatic changes in the body, mind and spirit of the growing adolescent demand a re-appraisal of their personal identity. Sexual freedom also implies enhanced personal independence and an opportunity to explore personal relationships in an intimate way.

Marcia's elaboration of Erikson's identity theory

Marcia (1994) has conceptually elaborated and empirically tested the stages of Erikson's identity theory. The operationalization of the key concepts and subsequent empirical work has resulted in some 300 studies on the topic (see Marcia *et al.,* 1993). An interview schedule was devised to explore the domains of occupational choice, ideology (religious and political beliefs) and interpersonal values, including 'sex role' attitudes and sexuality. The aim was to discover young people's exploration of these domains and their possible commitment to their choices. Marcia identified four major identity statuses: *Identity Diffusion, Foreclosure, Moratorium* and *Identity Achievement. Identity Diffusion* is marked by a lack of commitment; *Foreclosure* implies taking on ascribed views of parents and of 'significant others' without exploration; *Moratorium* is the state when issues are being explored and no commitment has yet been made (also referred to as *identity crisis*); and *Identity Achievement* results in firm commitments after exploration of issues. Marcia describes in some detail the behaviour pattern likely to be found in young people at each stage. Jean Phinney (1989) has adapted Marcia's model to study the ethnic identities of minority groups in the US and I will review her research presently.

The Foreclosure status of identity development needs further discussion as it mirrors quite closely the identity status of most of the first generation Asians, and should be of value in understanding the identity of their offspring. Marcia (1994) lists some of the features of people at this identity status:

Some of their experimentally determined characteristics are that they are authoritarian (they prefer to be told what to do by an acceptable authority rather than determining their own direction); set very high goals for themselves . . .; are somewhat inflexible in their thought processes; tend to espouse moral values at the level of law and order; . . . are generally obedient and conforming . . . they report, and their families report, a great deal of closeness and warmth.
(Marcia, 1994, p. 74)

At the risk of some simplification, it is suggested that this is a fairly good description of the behaviour pattern of the majority of first generation Asians from a rural background. In these rural areas, one's personal identity was derived and closely tied to one's kith and kin and community. For example, most young people followed in their parents' footsteps as far as their occupation was concerned and, likewise, their 'world views' were shaped by their religion and the community's belief system. Relationships within a family – and indeed the community as a whole – were based on patriarchy (father and male dominated) and on seniority of age[ii], and marriages were arranged.

What follows from this description is that the first generation may have (had) little sympathy with their offspring's predicament of identity exploration because of the nature of their own experience. However, we must also bear in mind that Marcia's model has been developed and tested in a European setting and its validity in explaining the nature of adolescence in other cultures may be deemed controversial. However, some Indian psychologists (Kakar, 1982; Sinha, 1996) argue that Eriksonian stages of development are similar to the ones found in ancient Hindu texts (*Mahabharata, Rigveda,* and *Dharamshastra*). The following quotation gives a flavour of Kakar's argument:

Daksha's opinion is shared by many authors: 'Till a boy is eight years old he is like one newly born and only indicates the caste in which he is born. As long as his upanayana *ceremony is not performed the boy incurs no blame as to what is allowed or forbidden.' The rituals of* jatakarman, annaprasana, *and* caula, *roughly coinciding with the beginnings of the first three Eriksonian stages, indicate a certain awareness of the turning points in the first three years of life.*
(Kakar, 1982, p. 7)

Development of ethnic awareness

The above discussion of ego identity leads us to consider the nature of the ethnic identity of young people in the UK. At this juncture, it may be judicious to consider some definitions of ethnic identity. Tajfel (1981) defines ethnic identity as 'that part of an individual's self-concept which derives from his knowledge of his membership of a social group (or groups) together with the value and emotional significance attached to that membership' (p. 255). Other definitions and interpretations of ethnicity include: self-identification; feelings of belongingness and commitment; and the sense of shared values and attitudes (see Phinney, 1990).

Milner (1983) argues that the development of ethnic identity takes the same route as the learning of gender and age-related roles. Role is defined as a set of behavioural responses expected from one who occupies a certain social position. Thus boys and girls are generally expected to behave differently from each other as are older children from younger ones. The basic means of transmission of the values, attitudes and skills of the society is through the process of socialization in the family. Other influences include the neighbourhood, street and, later on, the school. The media, especially TV, play their part in reinforcing certain parental values, although there is no conclusive evidence to substantiate this conjecture. According to Milner (1983, p. 60), 'A multicultural society creates realities which demand a heightened awareness of particular attitudes and identities. Here children come to view the world through race tinted spectacles, whether they are black or white'. There are many examples to substantiate his argument (Troyna and Hatcher, 1992; Wright, 1992). The response of an Indian-origin primary school boy, who was asked to tell us what it means to be British (*see* Ghuman, 1997), illustrates this:

Well, OK . . . someone that can speak a lot of English and would have white skin and different colour eyes and hair. Indian people have black hair and brown eyes.
(Ghuman, 1997, p. 71)

Differences in colour of hair and skin, facial features and dress are easily recognizable features by which the young child (at approximately three years old) can differentiate between him or herself and children of other ethnic groups. When this is established, children begin to identify with their own ethnic group (in-group) and show some dislike or rejection of other ethnic groups. These likes and dislikes (at around the age of five) of the other ethnic groups are internalized from the adults in their life.

Davey (1983) conducted a large-scale investigation into the ethnic awareness and attitudes of Asian, white and black children in England. He used a comprehensive range of tests, for example, expressing a preference for dolls by giving sweets to different coloured dolls, with children in the five- to seven-year-old age range. In general, he confirms the findings of Milner's research on the ethnic awareness of children at a very young age, but, in contrast to previous researchers, found that ethnic minority children do not reject their own group. Davey concludes the findings of his research:

In contrast with many earlier studies, which have stressed the importance of own-group rejection by minority group children, our findings demonstrate that both majority and minority group children have a strong sense of group identity. On the other hand, the pattern of ethnic group preferences showed that the minority children clearly perceived the advantages of being white.
(Davey, 1983, p. 173)

Furthermore, Davey notes that by the age of seven children's own group identification (ethnocentricity) was clearly established and there was little difference on account of sex, the ethnic mix of the school attended or the location (south/north) of place within the UK. He found that white children are significantly more ethnocentric (generally in favour of their own group) than Asian and black children, and that older children, with the exception of Asians, were less ethnocentric.

Most of the studies on ethnicity in the UK have been concerned, with a few exceptions, with primary school children (aged five to 11). Hutnik (1991) investigated the ethnic awareness and orientation of 14- to 16-year-old Indian, English and West Indian boys and girls through paper and pencil tests. In one of the tests, young people were asked to describe themselves. Cues were provided: namely, 'I am . . .'; and 'I am not . . .'. The author found 'that ethnic consciousness is significantly more salient in each minority group than in the English group, although on different dimensions' (p. 91). The two dimensions often chosen by Indian boys and girls to describe themselves were those of religion and being 'Indian'. This the researcher attributes to the prevailing prejudice and discrimination in Britain against Asian and black people.

To test her conjecture that ethnicity for the Indian-origin boys and girls is salient only in the British context, she replicated her study with a comparable sample in India. It was found that a significantly higher proportion of young people in Britain, irrespective of their social class, used 'Indian' to describe themselves in 'I am . . .' tests compared with their counterparts in India. Hutnik (1991) concludes: 'We have seen that South Asian adolescents in Britain are more aware of their ethnicity than are English or Indian adolescents, and this is probably because they constitute an ethnic minority group within the British society' (p. 95). In a subsequent investigation, Hutnik confirmed a modified version of Mcguire *et al.'s* hypothesis (1978) that ethnicity is a salient factor only when an ethnic group has a distinctive presence (that is, it is politically and socially significant). This has an important bearing on our discussion of Chinese young people in Britain. The Chinese community is too geographically spread out to form a coherent group and to develop cultural and religious institutions to form and maintain its distinctiveness. Therefore Chinese young people show less consciousness of their ethnicity than do their Hindu, Muslim and Sikh counterparts (Modood *et al.*, 1997).

In another follow-up study, Hutnik (1991) established that, out of the two components of ethnicity (religion and being 'Indian'), religion was the more central to young people's identity. Another seminal finding of the study was that '. . . the results [of Study 5] do not support the idea that ethnic minority individuals are burdened with feelings of self-hatred' (p. 107). This point will be taken up later when a discussion on the self-esteem of Asian young people is presented. In summarizing the results of all her investigations, Hutnik concludes: '. . . ethnicity is not a very salient component relative to other components of identity, such as Psychic style and Inter-personal style' (p. 108). Nevertheless, she argues that ethnicity might become more salient in adulthood when individuals have to make choices in the field of housing and employment, where a degree of discrimination exists. This conclusion, and indeed others, should be treated with some caution as the numbers in the samples are very small indeed and the tests used have no reliability and validity data to evaluate their merit. Furthermore, the wording of questions/ statements is problematic in this type of research and can affect the responses given. Nonetheless, her studies with young adolescents break new ground in empirical investigation into ethnicity and identity. There is a corpus of work on the ethnic identity of young people in North America by Phinney and his associates and I will now turn to their research.

Phinney's contribution

Phinney has applied Marcia's model to explain the development of ethnic identity in minority-group adolescents. Whilst the research is of great interest both from conceptual and pragmatic perspectives, its findings and application to the UK and the European scenes are not without problems. The understanding of identity and its structure, and indeed other related issues of prejudice and discrimination, have to be rooted within the socio-cultural milieu and political *zeitgeist* of a country. As has been commented upon by several researchers, social psychologists tend to be dismissive, or even ignorant, of wider historical and contemporary societal forces impinging upon the individual (Hutnik, 1991; Louch, 1966).

Phinney (1989) argues that in the Identity Diffusion status, there is a lack of interest in, or concern with, ethnicity; at the Foreclosure status, ethnicity is based upon the unexamined views of parents and of significant others; at the Moratorium status (ethnic identity search), there is an attempt to explore and to understand for oneself the meaning of ethnicity; and, at Identity Achievement status, there crystallizes a clear and confident sense of one's own ethnicity. Of course, the Identity Achievement status may give way to the Moratorium status again if a re-think of one's ethnic identity is undertaken whether intentionally or unintentionally. This is termed a moratorium–achievement–moratorium–achievement (MAMA) cycle (Stephen *et al.*, 1992).

Phinney (1989) developed criteria from Marcia's identity statuses which are applicable to the study of ethnicity. These can be summarized as:

Diffuse: *Little or no exploration of one's ethnicity, and no clear understanding of the issues.*
Foreclosed: *Little or no exploration of ethnicity, but apparent clarity about one's own ethnicity. Feelings about one's ethnicity may be either positive or negative, depending on one's socialisation experiences.*
Moratorium: *Evidence of exploration, accompanied by some confusion about the meaning of one's own ethnicity.*
Achieved: *Evidence of exploration, accompanied by a clear, secure understanding and acceptance of one's own ethnicity.*
(Phinney, 1989, p. 38)

These conceptually developed explanations were used by Phinney and her co-workers to test the model with a sample of Asian-American, Black, Hispanic and white high school adolescents (aged 15 to 17). All the young people in the study were interviewed using 20 questions from Marcia's ego identity interview, but these questions were specifically focused on ethnicity. For example, one of the questions was: 'Have you ever thought about whether your ethnic background will make a difference in your life as an adult?' The findings of this well-planned research revealed that the ethnic minority young people in the study did exhibit the three identity stages, namely, Foreclosure, Moratorium and Achievement. But the white American youths did not show evidence of any of these stages, except that they considered themselves Americans. Furthermore, there was little evidence to support the view that ethnic minorities, with the exception of Asian-American students, tend to have negative attitudes towards their own group. The author attributes this exception to the fact that Asian-Americans tend towards assimilation, rather than some form of bi-culturalism or pluralism which is usual to the other groups.

Phinney (1989) summarizes some other aspects of her research:

*Minority group membership per se did not affect adjustment . . .
However, those minority adolescents who had explored and were
aware about the meaning of their ethnicity (ethnic identity
achieved) showed higher scores on self-evaluation, sense of
mastery, social and peer interactions, and family relations,
compared to the diffusion and foreclosed adolescents.*
(Phinney, 1989, p. 47)

Phinney and Alipuria (1990) report that ethnic minority students
rate ethnicity as a central identity concern, very close to religion and
above politics. In another investigation, Phinney and Rosenthal
(1987) found that adolescents think the resolution of ethnicity-related
issues to be of importance. Phinney (1989) summarizes the research
of other scholars and concludes that ethnicity has been an important
factor in the development of ego identity. Another longitudinal study
(see Phinney and Chavira, 1995) was conducted with a sample of
18 adolescents from three groups of ethnic minority adolescents.
The aim was to verify the development of ethnic identity from the
stage of Foreclosure through Moratorium to Achievement. The young
people in the study were interviewed at age 16 and again three years
later. Overall, the authors confirm the progression of ethnic identity
and found that self-esteem (assessed independently) was significantly
correlated with ethnic identity at each period and across the three-year
time span. The authors suggest that strong support from the family
may be an important factor implicated in the development of mature
ethnic identity. The study has some weaknesses in that it was carried
out with a small self-selected sample (one third of the original) and
that the interviews were held over the telephone. Nevertheless, it
adds to our understanding of the nature of ethnic identity and its
significance in the life of adolescents.

Phinney's Multigroup Ethnic Identity Measure

In-depth interviewing, which has been used by Phinney and her
co-workers, is a very time-consuming method of collecting data. For
this reason, the numbers in their studies were small and, furthermore,
there are problems relating to the reliability and validity of the data.
To overcome these shortcomings, Phinney (1992) devised a scale[iii]
(the *Multigroup Ethnic Identity Measure – MEIM*) and tested its
suitability with a large number (n = 417; age range 14–19 years) of
different ethnic minority young people in the US. It consists of 14
items and covers three aspects of ethnic identity: *positive ethnic*

attitudes and sense of belonging (five items); *ethnic identity achievement* (seven items); *ethnic behaviour and practices* (two items). However, the factor analysis (a statistical technique to discover the composition of the scale) of the scores revealed only one factor of ethnic identity for the whole scale. There are other matters of interest: 'these results suggest that ethnic identity may become more consolidated with age ... evidence of progress toward ethnic identity achievement between the ages of 16 and 19 years' (p. 170). The author found no differences in 'ethnicity' due to social class or gender. The self-rated high academic achievers scored significantly higher compared with those who rated themselves as average and low achievers. Furthermore, the minority groups showed significantly higher scores than did the whites – the black students scoring the highest.

In a subsequent follow-up study, Phinney and her co-workers (Roberts *et al.*, 1997) tested the scale with a very large sample of young adolescents (aged 10–17 years, n = 5423) belonging to 20 different ethnic groups in the US. In addition, they explored the association of ethnicity with other factors such as self-esteem, psychological wellbeing and depression. To validate the scale, the researchers also used a single item on 'ethnic salience', namely, how important the students' ethnic background was to them. The factor analysis revealed two factors in contrast to the single factor in the research discussed previously (Phinney, 1992). The first major factor (which explains 33 per cent of the variance and loads on seven items) is composed of items which reflect 'feelings of attachment and belonging to a group'. The second factor (which explains 10 per cent of the variance and loads on five items) describes the 'exploration and learning aspects of ethnicity'. As regards the validity of the scale (that is, how far it really measures ethnic identity), the researchers found that the scores on the scale showed significant positive correlations with measures of psychological wellbeing (namely, coping, mastery, self-esteem, optimism and happiness) and negative correlations with loneliness and depression. Also, there was a significant positive correlation between the scores on the scale and 'saliency of ethnicity'. All these indices therefore demonstrate that the scale (*MEIM*) is a valid measure of ethnic identity. The researchers conclude:

It seems clear from this study that the concept of ethnic identity is meaningful for young adolescents, and that it is related in theoretically meaningful ways to other dimensions of the adolescents' experience ... It remains to be demonstrated how ethnic identity is related to the wider experience of adolescents,

for example their ethnic socialisation, the ethnic context in which they live, and the attitudes of the community toward a particular group.
(Phinney, 1992, p. 8)

This conclusion is somewhat at variance with that of Hutnik (1991), who argued from the findings of her investigations that 'ethnicity' is not a very salient component relative to other components of identity. It appears, therefore, that further investigations with a variety of measures (both of Phinney's and Hutnik's) should clarify the situation. Overall, Phinney and her co-workers' contribution – which is both quantitative and qualitative – has been significant in understanding the nature of ethnic identity and other associated concepts. Now we turn our attention to the two important topics of acculturation and bi-culturalism.

Acculturation and bi-culturalism

Acculturation

Acculturation may be defined as the process by which immigrants adopt the way of life of their host society. Some scholars refer to this process as that of *enculturation* (see Weinreich, 1985). At one polar end of the acculturation continuum we can have immigrants who make minimum adjustment (*accommodation*) to their lifestyles, and at the other end of the polarity we have complete absorption (*assimilation*); and, between these two, integration, where a kind of bi-culturalism emerges.

Berry's (1994) model of acculturation was critically discussed in *Chapter 2*. Within Berry's (1997) framework, the first generation Asians in the UK were generally employing the 'separation' strategy of adaptation. The chief reason for this situation was that they had different languages, religions, family values and general lifestyles. The research evidence on the second generation throws up a complex picture of adaptation and consequent lifestyles.

The Aberystwyth Bi-culturalism Scale

The writer has carried out several investigations (Ghuman, 1994; 1995a,b; 1996; 1997) on the South Asian younger generation using both qualitative (semi-structured interviews) and quantitative (attitude scale) methods. A Likert-type attitude scale was devised in the early 1970s (Ghuman, 1975) in which the respondent is asked to express his or her degree of agreement or otherwise, on a five-point scale.

Ninety-four items relating to the adolescents' own culture and to English culture were assembled in the area of: food and clothes; women's roles; values and beliefs; leisure and entertainment; general lifestyles. These were given to 16 'judges' (eight South Asians and eight English knowledgeable persons who rated the acculturation statements on seven points, according to their judgement) for their comments and suggestions. Following their comments, only forty items were retained after an extensive revision and then these were pilot tested on a small number of adolescents. The scale was subsequently reduced to 34 items, and then given to 86 boys and girls aged 14 to 16 years. Item analysis of the scale was carried out by the standard procedure (Likert, 1932), which yielded 30 items – 16 relating to the English way of life and 14 sampling the adolescents' opinion on their own culture. Subsequently another two items on the English way of life were added to bring it up-to-date. Some of the items were negatively phrased to avoid the possible development of a desirable response-set: for example, the boys and girls giving a 'favourable' response to all the items. The full scale is to found in Ghuman (1997; see also the *Appendix* to this book) and a sample of items follows:

Values and beliefs: Parents and children should live on their own and not with grandparents and uncles.
We should always try to fulfil our parents' wishes.

Role of Women: Our women should wear Western clothes.
A woman's place is in the home.

Food: Sometimes we should cook English food in our homes.
I would rather eat our own food all the time.

Leisure: We should be allowed to meet each other in Youth Clubs.
Marriages should be arranged by the family.

The scale has been used with South Asian boys and girls aged 14–17 years on three separate occasions in Birmingham, UK (Ghuman, 1975; 1991a; 1994; 1997) and once in Vancouver, Canada (Ghuman, 1994). The scale has proved to be of high reliability (that is, consistency ranges from 0.83 – 0.9) and validity, as tested by the 'extreme group method' (see Burroughs, 1971). As the findings of these studies have been reported in detail elsewhere only a summary is presented here.

In the latest research (Ghuman, 1997), the scoring of the items was not reversed as in the earlier investigations, where items expressing a favourable opinion to 'acculturation' were scored high, for example, 'strongly agree', 5; 'agree', 4 and vice versa. The factor analysis of the data revealed two 'bipolar' factors. The first factor is named 'Acculturation', which accounts for 25 per cent of the variance (differences in scores) and the second, 'Traditionalism', which explains 11 per cent of the variance. The scores on these two factors were then used to discuss gender, social class and 'religious affiliation' differences.

The overall findings from the research undertaken by the writer have clearly demonstrated that girls show more willingness to acculturate (measured by higher scores on the acculturation factor) than do boys and that Hindu young people are more in favour of taking up English values and way of life than are Muslims. Sikh young people come somewhere in-between Hindus and Muslims as judged by their performance on the scale. The middle-class (based on the Registrar General Classification of Occupation 1, 2, 3A used in Britain) youngsters scored higher than their 'working class' counterparts. Predictably, a sample of boys and girls who were tested in the mid-1980s scored significantly higher on acculturation than an equivalent group in the mid-1970s, showing that young people who were born here or had their schooling in Britain are more in tune with the British way of life. Overall, the scores of young people on the scale suggest that they have a favourable attitude to acculturation.

Interestingly, though, the teenagers do not want to reject *all* aspects of their culture. They are keen to retain the key elements of their parents' culture as expressed in their response to those items on the scale. For example, they reject such items as 'Only Asian doctors can understand our illnesses' and 'Prefer to eat our own food' but express agreement with 'Should learn to read and write our language' and 'Should attend our places of our worship'. It became clear from the responses that they favour some form of bi-culturalism or, in Berry's (1997) terminology, 'integration'. This research has been conducted with relatively small samples and it is not claimed that these are representative of the wider population. Therefore we should now examine the findings of a large scale research.

Acculturation as preferred strategy

A national survey of opinion on the identity-related issues was published recently (Modood *et al.*, 1997). It showed that over two-thirds of the young people in the sample preferred the 'Accultura-tive' (integration) mode of adaptation, thus providing support for the writer's (Ghuman, 1994; 1995a; 1997) investigations. Likewise, Hutnik (1991), whose research was discussed earlier in this chapter, found that the most preferred strategy amongst Indian boys and girls was that of acculturation. She writes: 'It would seem that the majority of second generation Indian adolescents have learned to affirm effectively both the ethnic minority group and the majority group in this sample of cultural adaptation variables' (p. 128). Hutnik, however, suggests that the bipolar model (assimilation – separation/ dissociative) of studying young people's adaptation is oversimplified and should be replaced by a four-dimensional one in which a distinction should be made between positively liking one's ethnic culture and rejecting it, and positively liking the majority culture and rejecting it. This conclusion is based on the research methodology used by the author (respondents were given an either/or choice of items between the minority culture and the majority culture), but no conceptual analysis of the issues is presented to support this claim.

The fact that the majority of young people prefer integration to other modes of adaptation (for example, assimilation, marginalization and separation) is reinforced by the face-to face interview data (Ghuman, 1991b; 1994; 1995a;) obtained on such matters as language(s) spoken at home, choice of clothes, Asian music and videos, and vocational aspirations. In the first study (Ghuman, 1991b), it was found that a large majority of young people are bi-cultural and bilingual: they have retained some aspects of their own culture and at the same time adopted some of the British norms. Likewise, the majority define their personal identity in a 'hyphenated way' (for example, Indo-English). The boys in the study generally enjoyed more freedom than did the girls in the choice of clothes and going out and were generally shown preference by their parents – which caused much discontent amongst girls. Furthermore, most of the boys and girls in the study placed a high value on formal schooling and education, a recurring finding of research both in the UK, North America and Australia (Bhachu, 1985a, b; Tomlinson, 1984; Ogbu, 1994; Bullivant, 1987).

A comparative study by the present author (Ghuman, 1994) of South Asian boys and girls in Britain and Canada provides another perspective on acculturation. The young people in Vancouver appeared to be more enthusiastic in adopting Canadian lifestyles, with many of them opting for Canadian identity rather than Indian or hyphenated, and less keen to retain their community languages. They wanted to omit Sikh middle names (*Singh* for boys and *Kaur* for girls) and to anglicize their names. More importantly, they felt that they would hardly meet any racial prejudice in employment, which is in marked contrast to the second generation young people in Britain. The major reason for this lies probably in the difference between the socio-political climate of the two countries. Canadian society, on the whole, is more pluralistic and open and has been less hostile to its post-war immigrants compared with the British (Buchignani *et al.*, 1985). The comparison between the two groups brought out the saliency of socio-political factors in promoting, or retarding, integration of ethnic minority young people.

Stopes-Roe and Cochrane's studies

The studies of Stopes-Roe and Cochrane (1990; 1992) in the UK on older adolescents (aged between 18 and 21) of Indian and Pakistani origin are of great value and significance in that the planning of their investigations was very methodical. The samples chosen were large and representative of the target population, and a comparative white group was included as were the parents of all the offspring. In-depth interviews of the young people by ethnic minority language speakers has added further authenticity to their research. Furthermore, the sample included dyads (for example, mother and daughter and son and father) from the first and second generations.

Use of English

They found that the younger people had a greater degree of social contact with whites than did their parents. The largest difference between the two generations was in the use of English: the younger people conversed in English, especially with their siblings and friends. Such a practice discouraged parents from participation in their offspring's lives. For this reason, parents wanted their young people to learn their mother tongue and they thought that schools should be involved. The role of religion for both generations was paramount. The authors write: 'Secondly, a majority in both generations felt an obligation to keep their religion alive and pass it on to the future; and almost all of them saw this duty as belonging to their own community, although parents were more inclined than young people to involve schools as well' (p. 196).

Personal identity

On personal identity, the researchers found a significant shift in the younger generation: over one in ten (43.3 per cent) of them identified with Britain, whereas none of the parents thought this way. However, there is an interesting caveat to this: on further analysis the researchers found that, of those who identified with Britain, three-quarters also felt that there were differences between themselves and the white British. This is interpreted not as an indication of alienation, but rather as being associated with their distinctive cultural customs and the fact that they 'saw themselves at some disadvantage'. However, this could be due to the phrasing and form of the question asked of the respondents, which gave only two alternatives – British or Indian/Pakistani. The subjects were not given a third choice of bi-cultural identity (hyphenated), for example, Indo-English or British-Pakistani.

Inter-racial relationships

It is interesting to note that in their research (Stopes-Roe and Cochrane, 1990), a majority of the unmarried young people were not against the idea of inter-racial marriage, but two-thirds of the sample said that they would marry within their own community. Furthermore, most of the unmarried young people were not in revolt against their parents. The researchers found the young people to be very positively inclined towards maintaining family ties:

There is no evidence from our young people that they wanted, much less intended, to lose or even loosen their family ties. All they wanted was some freedom to come and go and socialise a bit more as they pleased, and to have their parents listen to their arguments . . . They had no wish to give up their families, only to have some life outside them.
(Stopes-Roe and Cochrane, 1990, p. 201–202)

On inter-generational conflict, the research found that half the South Asian and a third of the British dyads (parents–son/daughter) showed the potential for serious disagreements and discord over such matters as training, job, marriage and where to live. On the question of racial prejudice, the authors found that the British parents rationalized their attitudes by concealing them within their common sense observations, namely, Asians are numerous, energetic and successful and are perceived by whites to be their competitors in jobs, housing and in other walks of life. The white youngsters, however, showed less prejudice and were also more optimistic about the future of race-relations in the UK.

Recent research

The fieldwork for this research was carried out some ten years ago in the British Midlands. Let us, therefore, now turn to a more recent research (Moodod *et al.*, 1994) which used ethnographic procedures and was conducted in London, Birmingham and Leicester. A total of 49 second generation young people of South Asian origin were interviewed in a face-to-face situation in order to explore their attitudes towards their community languages, religion and identity. The whole approach to the study was qualitative. One of the salient findings was that religion still plays an important part in defining their ethnicity. The authors write:

71

In the second generation of every group studied here there is a strong sense of ethnic pride, of wanting to know about or at least to affirm one's roots in the face of a history and a contemporary society in which one's ethnicity has been suppressed or tainted with inferiority . . . Its [religion] significance here is that even those young Asians who do not practise their religion nevertheless recognise that religion as part of their distinctive heritage and ethnic identity . . .
(Modood *et al.*, 1994, p. 59)

A few young people described themselves as 'Asians' but they are only too well aware of the differences in religion, language, dress codes, diet and country of origin between the various groups from the Indian sub-continent. A Gujurati Hindu reply is typical of the Gujaratis in the study: 'There is a great deal of difference between a Gujarati and, say, a Punjabi. Their clothing is more expensive. They wear more jewellery. I cannot find many similarities between our cultures' (Modood *et al.*, 1994, p. 93). The generic label 'Asians' is perceived by the respondents to be imposed by the indigenous whites, and to be based largely on skin colour. The remark of a second generation Punjabi is illustrative: 'Whites who are racist see me as a "Paki", others that don't know me as an "Asian"' (Modood *et al.*, p.94). However, a few suggested that they might have to come to terms with this ascribed identity of being an 'Asian' or even Black and forge a common front to combat discrimination.

The researchers discuss at some length the young peoples' responses to the notion of 'Britishness'. More than half of the respondents felt themselves to a large extent to be culturally British. This was supported by reference to their appearance, forms of socializing and choice of entertainment. However, they felt strongly that they were still not accepted by white British. The rest of the group argued for some form of bi-culturalism because they felt that the white British are reluctant to accept cultural differences and consequently there is always pressure on them to minimize their ethnic identity. Several young people used hyphenated labels (for example, British-Pakistanis) to describe their identity. A few respondents rejected 'being British' on the grounds that they have an ethnically distinct religion and culture and therefore do not feel at ease with the indigenous whites. Overall, it becomes clear from reading the extracts of interviews that the respondents would prefer some form of bi-culturalism. And this is reflected in the researchers' conclusions:

Most of the second generation wanted to retain some core heritage, some amalgam of family cohesion, religion and language,

probably in an adapted form, but did not expect this to mean
segregated social lives, for they lived and wanted to live in an
ethnically mixed way.
(Modood *et al.*, 1994, p. 110)

This is a small scale research with many shortcomings: small sample; subjective interpretation of the data; and an omission of the important variable of social class. But its findings concur with the results of other researchers discussed earlier in this chapter and therefore adds to our understanding of the crucial concept of ethnic identity as used and 'lived' by Asian youth.

It is instructive to compare the findings of these studies with that of an American study. Gibson (1988) used an anthropological approach (advocated by Ogbu, 1994) to study the adaptation strategies and educational attainment of the Punjabi Sikhs in California. Her research findings are wide-ranging and will be discussed later, but on identity she found: ' . . . Punjabi young people remained firmly and squarely anchored in their Punjabi identity. Like their parents they reacted negatively to the conformist pressures of the majority group'(p. 139). However, young people, unlike their parents, were in favour of acculturation and believed that this is possible without assimilation and losing one's identity. The researcher labels it as *accommodation without assimilation*. Accommodation to American cultural traditions and mores in practical terms would lead to some kind of bi-culturalism. Such a strategy is also the preferred way of the majority of South Asian young people in the UK, as noted previously in this chapter.

The identity of Chinese-origin young people

We will now discuss the identity of Chinese-origin young people. A well-planned research by Parker (1995) investigated this issue. In all, he studied 122 young people, nearly two-thirds of whom were born in Britain. He used a questionnaire and in-depth interview method to research, among other matters, ethnic identity. As a backdrop to the research, he notes the general attitudes held by the British towards the Chinese in the UK: 'Chinese can come here, keep their culture and prosper so long as they stay within their precise territories and don't compete with the bulk of society' (p.80).

'Take-aways' and restaurants

According to Parker, most of the first generation Chinese (Watson (1975) argues nearly 90 per cent) worked for long hours in 'take-aways' and restaurants. The younger generation's early experiences therefore are rooted in these places. Often their parents work in isolation from the other members of their communities because of the dispersed nature of their business. Most young people are called upon to help in the business (with long hours of late opening) after school, and this has shaped their attitudes to indigenous people and has also influenced the development of their personal and ethnic identities. Parker's own experience in a 'take-away' is instructive:

The overriding impression was how deeply the whole of family life was structured by the take-away, and how little time is consequently left for parents to develop meaningful relationships . . . there is no strongly binding religious tradition or act of collective worship to act as a symbolic focus for Chinese identity.
(Parker, 1995, p. 85–86)

Racism

Most young people in the study had faced racism when working in take-away shops. They had learnt to deal with it in their own unique way, but most of them said it made them aware, and proud, of being Chinese. The response of a girl in the study shows how distressing such psychological experiences can be:

When I was working in my parents' shop a 'customer' skitted at me real bad, so when I finished work I went upstairs, ripped all my Michael J. Fox posters, Tom Cruise, everything that had white skin and cried my eyes out. It made me so angry. I was quite young as well, probably about 14. It makes me sick thinking of it. But now, I've sort of learnt how to deal with it, because I'm proud of my race and not afraid to express myself.
(Parker, 1995, p. 100)

However, the minority of young people in the study who came from non-catering backgrounds expressed their disquiet at being stereo-typed as 'take-away' people. Nevertheless they also have encountered racism in schools and in other social situations.

Ethnic identity and language

A quarter of the respondents thought of themselves as Chinese. A third of the sample thought of themselves as British, and just under a third described their identities in a 'hyphenated' way, for example, as British-Chinese. The rest did not respond. To the question, 'How important is being of Chinese origin to you?', nearly three-quarters of the sample thought it to be very or quite important. It was noted in *Chapter 3* that the Chinese communities show less fervour for their religion than do the people from the Asian sub-continent, but they are keener to retain their mother tongue which, for the majority, is Cantonese. The researcher found that nearly two-thirds of them attended supplementary schools to learn Cantonese but only a fifth could read and write it. Consequently, it is suggested that, for most young people, Chinese Hong Kong culture – rather than the traditional Chinese – is absorbed through oral and visual sources rather than through the extended written form of Chinese. Parker (1995) argues that Hong Kong popular culture, as expressed in its films and videos, music, and clothes fashion, is having an increasing influence on the young Chinese in Britain, North America and elsewhere. Therefore, it is serving as an identity marker.

Eighty per cent of the young people in the study have been to visit their East Asian country of origin at least once, showing a continued active interest in their root culture. However, most of the respondents expressed some regret that, unlike Indian/Pakistani and African-Caribbean origin young people, they have failed to develop their own distinctive youth culture. This is attributed by the researcher to the lack of a critical mass of Chinese settlement in any one locality and to the narrowness within which 'to be Chinese' is defined.

Coping with culture conflict

To resolve the culture conflict caused by the dual allegiance to British and Chinese cultures, a range of solutions was adopted by the young Chinese. A small number of students within the sample resolved the conflict by choosing British identity. A few expressed strong disapproval of those who run down the British way of life: 'If they're that discontented with this country, they should go back to their own country and see how they get on there'. As a way of coping with racial prejudice and rejection, a few young people preferred a regional identity (for example, Northern) to British or English. By far the most frequently expressed opinion indicated that they have learnt to compartmentalize their experiences. A respondent amplified:

About half, half British and half Chinese . . . at home I'm a different person to how I am outside. At the weekend we live a Chinese life, at school it's very English. I think we get both the English entertainment and the Chinese as well . . . like having two kinds of cultures to go for.
(Parker, 1995, p. 193)

A few others in the group preferred to have Chinese identity as they were convinced that they would never be accepted by the British because of their cultural and physical differences. One response typifies their thinking: ' ... But to me, I say my nationality is British but I'm Chinese in identity and origin, my cultural background is Chinese'. These young people were of the opinion that one must have a firm sense of identity within a culture, otherwise one might be lacking a firm and secure personal identity.

There were several instances of young people who were at a moratorium stage of identity formation, that is, one expressing ambivalence whilst still exploring and enquiring. One of the respondents gave a very articulate view of her own feelings on the subject:

That is such a hard question. I do feel British; I do feel Anglo-Chinese; I do feel mixed I accept that; I know what it is to be English but I don't know what it is to be Chinese and that is part of my identity which I'm trying to expand. . . . I do feel it's moving and expanding my racial identity is also very much to do with my identity as a woman and also my sexual identity . . . my political identity. I can't separate them, they are all mixed up. (Parker, 1995, p. 198)

The usual weaknesses of small scale qualitative research are also to be found in this work but nevertheless it adds another piece to the jigsaw in understanding the complex and elusive notion of ethnic identity. A large-scale national survey of opinion on Asians in Britain (referred to earlier – Modood *et al.*, 1997) found that only 11 per cent of the Chinese young people in the sample thought 'Religion is very important to how I live my life' compared with 73 and 43 per cent respectively of the Pakistani and Indian young people. Fifteen of the 16 young British-born Chinese thought of themselves as being British. These findings need cautious interpretation as the researchers were working with a small number of young people and there is no discussion on the reliability or the 'face' validity of the responses. However, it seems that younger generation Chinese prefer an assimilation strategy to integration in their social adaptation (see Berry's model in this chapter), in contrast to their forefathers/ mothers. The other interesting finding is that all the sub-groups in the sample (Indian, Pakistani, Bangladeshi and Chinese) showed a decline in their ability to speak their respective mother tongues. For instance, in the case of the Chinese, 'just over four in ten of the 16- to 34-year-olds use Chinese language with family of their own age, and nearly a quarter of all respondents are not able to speak a Chinese (or Vietnamese) language' (Modood *et al.*, 1997, p. 312).

Phinney (1989) found that a significantly higher percentage of young people of Asian-American origin (which includes Chinese, Vietnamese and Japanese) wanted to be white – 53 per cent as opposed to around 10 per cent of the Blacks and Hispanics. She concludes that, on the whole, young people of Asian-American origin tend to prefer assimilation to integration, the latter being the preferred option of the other two groups in the study. However, in this context, it is important to note the research findings of Ying (1995) in San Francisco. The researcher found that bicultural Chinese individuals in the study enjoyed both Chinese and American cultural activities and reported a better wellbeing (as measured by four objective tests) than did their counterparts who stayed traditional, or favoured assimilation into the mainstream.

Weinreich's *Identity Structure Analysis*

The *Identity Structure Analysis* (*ISA*) was developed by Weinreich (1989) to study identity-related issues by providing an interdisciplinary conceptual framework and by formulating operational definitions of the key concepts used in the analysis. This model can be used cross-culturally in that the socio-historical and cultural contexts can be embodied in its empirical procedures. The author states such a claim for the model: 'It enables the investigation of the uniqueness of each ethnic group, while making it possible to draw general conclusions that hold across groups, dependent as these conclusions will be on the given historical circumstances of the relationships among groups' (p. 111). The basic assumption of the model is that the concept of the 'self' is situated within the social context of the family and the broader community within which one lives. A second assumption is that the concept of identity is not a linear one (that is, defined by self-esteem, identity conflict or social identity) but multifaceted and that these components modulate from context to context.

Use of the **ISA** *with Pakistani-origin young people*

The *ISA* has been used by Kelly and Weinreich (1986) to study the identity-related issues of Pakistani-origin young people in the UK. In their study, the subjects were 20 Pakistani Muslim women aged 16–21 years; a comparable sample of indigenous British women was also included. Based on the respondents' values, the researchers identified two groups in the sample: 'Progressive' and 'Orthodox'. The Progressive women subscribed to such values as choice of marriage partner, outside work, and tolerance of other religions, whereas, conversely, the Orthodox women preferred adherence to traditional arranged marriages, staying at home and a strong attachment to Islam. The authors found that the Progressive group perceived themselves as having much more in common with British people than did the Orthodox group and, consequently, the former showed higher levels of conflict in 'identification' than did the latter.

Use of the ISA with Chinese-origin young people

Weinreich *et al.* (1996) investigated the ethnic identity and acculturation of Hong Kong Chinese students by using the *ISA* methodology. The findings of this study are rather complex (and the reader is referred to the original article) but the implications for the study of 'acculturation' are interesting. The researchers argue that 'acculturation' often implies modification of a more 'primitive' culture through contact with an 'advanced' culture and is thus used to refer to people with minority status. They propose instead the concept of 'enculturation', which would enable the study of 'culture-change' through the incorporation of cultural elements (both minority and majority) as opposed to change towards the dominant culture. This would appear to be a useful notion because it does allow for the emergence of new cultural idioms. In Britain, there are innovations, as noted in previous chapters, in the field of music and literature and in many other walks of life. Support for such a perspective comes from a theoretical model proposed by La Fromboise *et al.* (1993). The researchers discuss five models of adaptation which the ethnic minority may utilize, namely, *Assimilation, Acculturation, Alternation, Multiculturalism*, and *Fusion*. They argue that, of all the perspectives, the *Alternation* (a form of bi-culturalism) optimizes the knowledge of the cultural beliefs and values of both groups, leads to bicultural efficacy, develops better communication through bilingualism and provides a sound anchoring for the minority groups.

Self-image, self-concept and self-esteem

Some researchers (Phinney and Rotheram, 1987) have linked the development of ethnic identity to self-esteem. It is apposite therefore to turn our attention to the discussion of self-esteem and a family of other concepts. Researchers have used the notions of 'self-concept' and 'self-image' in an interchangeable fashion, although some writers (see Wylie, 1974) would like to make an analytical distinction between the two. Self-concept is supposed to be an objective (cognitive) appraisal of oneself, whereas self-image implies the evaluation of one's *self*, that is, feelings of good or poor attached to it. In practice, however, there is little difference between the two as feelings and attitudes are invariably part and parcel of our categorization and labelling processes (see Bagley *et al.*, 1975).

Self-image, according to Coopersmith (1975) – whose question-naire has been used extensively in research, is generally understood to be 'the concept represented by the person's picture of himself to himself, and has been variously called the self-image, self, or self-concept' (p. 148). He argues that people not only form pictures of themselves but also develop and attach negative or positive feelings and attitudes (such as likes and dislikes, affection and hostility) to their self-image. Coopersmith's definition of self-image is built from these basic notions: 'these positive or negative attitudes and feelings about the self are the evaluative sentiments known as self-esteem' (p. 148). There are many other interpretations of self-esteem (see Bagley *et al.*, 1975; Wylie, 1974) and, indeed, different ways of operationalizing and assessing it but, in our brief review, we will pursue Coopersmith's conceptualization.

Pioneering research on the self-image (as reflected in ethnic identification tests) of black children was carried out in the US by, amongst others, Clark (1955) and Radke and Trager (1950). In these studies children were asked to choose between black and white dolls in response to the question: 'Give me the doll that looks like you.' The inference drawn from these studies is summarized thus:

One consequence of adopting these standards is that lighter skin colour, straight hair and narrow nose are preferred characteristics, i.e., features associated with whiteness are likely to be regarded as more attractive than the dark colour . . . Given a choice over two-thirds of black children prefer a light-skinned doll over a doll with dark skin colour'.
(p. 155)

The low self-esteem of black children was attributed to the general low status of black people in society (that is, before the dawn of the black consciousness movement in the 1960s) in that they were denied basic civil rights and equal educational and employment opportunities. James Baldwin (1964), the famous black novelist, wrote:

The women were forever straightening and curling their hair, and using bleaching creams. And yet it was clear that none of this effort would release one from the stigma and danger of being a Negro; this effort merely increased the shame and rage . . .
(Quoted in Milner, 1983, p. 147)

Positive images of black people in the US and of the former colonials (Asians, West Indians) in Britain began to emerge during the 1960s and have continued to do so to the present day. This renewed ethnic pride has been mainly instrumental in raising the self-image of ethnic minority children and young people, as will become clear from the following section.

The earlier studies in Britain (Milner, 1983) showed a degree of white-orientation in black and Asian children, as was noted with black children in the US. However, the post-1960s studies tell a different story. Davey (1983) concludes from his large scale study; 'The low frequency of misidentification by West Indian and Asian children, in fact, compares favourably with the incidence of misidentification amongst white children. These data are in marked contrast with those from many earlier studies . . .' (1983, p. 99). However, in the preference test (choosing out of three photographs which one the respondent would most like to be), 45 per cent of both the Asian and West Indian children chose a picture of a white person, whereas only a small percentage of the whites chose an Asian or a West Indian. The researcher attributes this to the children's perception 'as to who has the favoured place in the social pecking order'.

Louden (1978) studied the self-esteem of South Asian, West Indian and English adolescents in the British Midlands. He found no significant difference between the groups, but the girls in each of the ethnic groups had lower self-esteem than did the boys of that ethnic group. This is explained by invoking the cultural and social climate of the time, when girls generally were still given fewer opportunities compared with boys to develop their personal and intellectual skills. Milner (1983) summarizes the findings of studies on self-image: 'Most of these studies were conducted in the 1960s and early 1970s and demonstrated comparable levels of self-esteem in blacks and whites' (p. 155). Hutnik (1991), whose research was discussed in some detail earlier in this chapter, found no significant difference in self-esteem between Indian-origin and English boys and girls. Bagley, Mallick and Verma (1979) reviewed the literature on self-esteem and overall they reported no significant differences between the Asians and white teenagers, although there were minor variations relating to gender differences. A literature search on this topic revealed no major studies since the publication of this review in the UK.

Summary

One of the main findings to emerge from a literature survey on the identity of Asian young people is the saliency of ethnicity. Firstly, ethnicity seems to be rooted in religion and language, which in many instances is only symbolic in nature – the young people do not always practise their religion, nor are they learning to read and write their ancestral language. The emergence of ethnicity is largely attributed to two factors: in-group belongingness on the one hand, and the experience of exclusion from the mainstream, on the other.

Secondly, it emerges that ethnic identity develops as does the ego-identity, and that Marcia's model, as adapted by Phinney (1996a, b), is conceptually sound and a pragmatic procedure for understanding ethnicity and its associations with the family of other concepts.

Thirdly, it appears that a majority of the young people are learning to be bi-cultural and bilingual (more at a spoken level) and are prone to using 'hyphenated' identities for self-description. At one end of the 'assimilation–separation continuum' are the Chinese-origin young people, who are more likely to seek assimilation to the British way of life, while at the other end are the Pakistanis and Bangaldeshis who are prone to emphasize their distinctive Muslim identity and to seek merely a form of accommodation with their host culture. The young people of Indian background (including those who migrated from East Africa) are pursuing a 'middle way' of integration between the two cultures.

Finally, the research to date on the self-image of Asian young people does not show any significant difference between them and their white counterparts, except that Pakistani and Bangladeshi young people score slightly lower than Indians, who in turn score higher than other groups (Verma and Mallick, 1988).

Next to the family, schools are the most important institutions of socialization of children and young people. The 'nature' of schooling profoundly affects the development of ego identity and, indeed, ethnic identity. Schooling is compulsory up to the age of 16 in the UK and prepares young people for their adult roles. Examination success at school is of crucial importance as it opens the doors to higher education and to skilled jobs. It is vital, therefore, to discuss in some detail the effect of schooling on Asian young people's lives. The next chapter is devoted to the exploration of such issues.

Further reading (Chapters 3 and 4)

Aboud, F. (1988). *Children and Prejudice*. London: Basil Blackwell.
An all-round good review of theories of prejudice and a description of the author's social-cognitive theory of prejudice.

Ghuman, P. A. S. (1994). *Coping With Two Cultures: A study of British Asian and Indo-Canadian adolescents*. Clevedon: Multilingual Matters.
Chapter 2 deals with the acculturation of Asian young people.

Hutnik, N. (1991). *Ethnic Minority Identity in Britain: A Social Psychological Perspective*. Oxford: Clarendon Press.
Chapters 6 and 7 should be of interest to the reader.

Kroger, J. (1989). *Identity in Adolescence: The balance between self and other*. London: Routledge.
Chapters 1 and 2 are relevant to the discussion of issues raised in these two chapters.

Milner, D. (1983). *Children and Race – Ten Years On*. London: Wardlock Educational.
An excellent review of the literature on racial prejudice and identity studies.

Parker, D. (1995). *Through Different Eyes: The cultural identities of young Chinese people in Britain*. Aldershot: Avebury.
Chapters 5 and 6 deal with the identity-related issues of Chinese young people in the UK.

Phinney, S. and Rotheram, J. M. (1987). *Children's Ethnic Socialization: Pluralism and development*. London: Sage Publications.
A collection of papers on ethnicity of minority group children and young people from North America and Australia. Part III of the book is devoted to the exploration of ethnic identity in adolescence and later childhood and is recommended to readers.

Stopes-Roe, M. and Cochrane, R. (1990). *Citizens of this Country: The Asian-British*. Clevedon: Multilingual Matters.
Chapters 4, 7 and 8 are very informative. The book is based on an empirical study and adopts a social psychological perspective.

Taylor, J H. (1976). *The Half-Way Generation*. Windsor: National Foundation for Educational Research.
A dated but lucid account of Asian youths in Newcastle, England.

---

i Examples of formal thinking are to be found in Peel's 1971 book. Young people are given a passage to read and are then asked to answer questions on the cause of the stated problems . The correct solution lies in considering many alternative explanations rather than just 'Yes' or 'No' answers.

ii The reader is cautioned that since the 1960s there have been radical economic and industrial changes in Asian countries which have caused social mobility, and this description may not quite fit. Hence the description in the past tense.

iii The respondents were invited to express their opinion on a 4-point scale ranging through 'strongly agree', 'somewhat agree', 'somewhat disagree' to 'strongly disagree'. Items included: 'I have a clear sense of my ethnic background and what it means to me' and 'I have a strong sense of belonging to my own ethnic group'.

5

Schools and Asian Young People

It is a complex pursuit of fitting a culture to the needs of its members and of fitting its members and their ways of knowing to the needs of the culture.
(Bruner, 1996, p. 43)

The first generation of Asian people migrated to Britain, the United States and elsewhere primarily to improve their standard of living and thereby to benefit their kith and kin back home. Another motive for settling in the UK was to enable their offspring to avail themselves of the excellent educational opportunities. The education system of the UK was, and still is, held in very high regard, primarily due to the former imperial connections. Therefore, their permanent settlement in Britain would hopefully secure the first and subsequent generations advantages which would otherwise be open only to the elite in their country of origin. These high expectations of the first generation were not always fully realized, due to a variety of complex psychological and sociological reasons.

In this chapter, the analysis and discussion concerns the development of basic cognitive processes and the examination performance and access to higher education of Asian young people. Other issues discussed include teachers' attitudes, inter-ethnic relationships, bilingualism and the position of Asian girls in schools.

Basic cognitive processes

Bruner (1996) argues that '. . . you cannot understand mental activity unless you take into account the cultural setting and its resources, the very things that give mind its shape and scope' (p. x). Research on the cognitive processes involving the thinking, reasoning and problem-solving abilities of Asian children and young people is sparse indeed. Of this, most of the extant research has been with children rather than adolescents.

One of the earliest studies was carried out in Glasgow, Scotland (Ashby *et al.*, 1970) to discover the effect of British schooling on the cognitive abilities of South Asian children. The researchers gave a comprehensive battery of tests to 11-year-old Indian and Pakistani-origin children and also included a comparative sample of indigenous Scottish whites. The tests included: *Glasgow* and *Moray House Verbal Reasoning, Goodenough Draw-a-man Test* and *Raven Matrices*. The findings of this research showed quite clearly that the Asian children who were either born in Britain or were of long-stay (nine or more years) performed as well as their white Scottish peers. The authors reinforced the findings of previous studies (Burgin and Edison, 1967; Saint, 1963) in that performance on tests is related to environmental factors rather than to the genetic make-up of children.

Impact of environmental factors

Ghuman (1975) extended the conceptual framework of cross-cultural research by including an indigenous sample from India. A battery of tests was given to British Punjabi boys (aged 10–11-years-old) in the British Midlands to find out if there were any differences in their thinking processes compared with those of their British counterparts. A comparable group of Punjabi boys from the Punjab was also included. The battery of tests included: *Raven Matrices, WISC Blocks*, Piagetian tests of Conservation of Mass, Weight, and Area, *Vygotsky Blocks* (test of concept formation) and a card sorting test. On all these tests, the performance of the Punjabi boys was similar to that of their British counterparts but both the groups were significantly superior in performance to that of the Punjabi group from the Punjab. The research showed the significant impact of the social milieu and schooling on the development of basic thinking processes. A follow-up study (Ghuman, 1978), which also included girls, confirmed the saliency of environmental factors even on the performance of generally accepted 'culture-free' tests such as the *Raven Matrices* and *Draw-a-man*. Vyas (1983) tested Gujarati children in Gujarat (India) and London on a variety of tests which included Piagetian tests and the *Children's Embedded Figures Test* (CEFT) – a test of analytical ability. His findings showed quite clearly that Gujarati children in London were scoring higher compared with their counterparts in Gujarat and were close to the European norms for the tests.

A recent study by the author (Ghuman, 1994) of Indian adolescents aged 14- to 16-years-old in Delhi showed their comparatively poor performance on a variety of Piagetian tests and tasks of logical reasoning. This was attributed to the poor quality of their schooling with its emphasis on rote learning and memory work.

An earlier comparative study by the author (Ghuman, 1980a) of cognitive styles using *Witkin's Field-Dependence/Independence Test* (and a maths and a spatial test) also showed the strong influence of schooling and the social milieu on reasoning abilities. The research was carried out in the British Midlands with a sample of young adolescents (aged 13- to 14-years-old) of Indian and Pakistani origin. A sample of British adolescents was also tested to provide a comparative perspective. It was hypothesized that British boys and girls would be more field-independent than their Asian peers because of British child-rearing practices. As discussed in *Chapter 2* of this book, Witkin (1966) linked the development of analytical thinking ability to independence training in early infancy and childhood which British parents tend to emphasize in contrast to the traditional attitudes of Indian and Pakistani parents. However, in this research, there was no difference between the two groups on the field-dependent/independent and the spatial tests, although the Asian children performed better than did the British children on the mathematical achievement test. It was argued that the effect of schooling may be more salient and pervasive than that of the early upbringing. Such a contention is supported by Wagner (1982) who came to a similar conclusion from his research with Mexican children in the US. It is important to bear in mind that these studies are not experimental, and use small numbers of boys and girls, and therefore they can only point out trends, rather than facilitate broad generalizations.

The National Foundation for Educational Research team (Taylor and Hegarty, 1985) reviewed the research extant until 1984 on cognitive abilities and came to the following conclusion:

This 20-year review of research on the assessment of ability of pupils of Asian origin has charted methodological changes, from employing IQ tests to verbal, later non-verbal and more recently learning and cognitive ability tests . . . Indeed there is considerable cumulative evidence that the performance of pupils of Asian origin increases with length of schooling so that recent research shows that by the end of their primary years the intellectual abilities of those with full schooling, as measured by conventional tests, approaches those of their British peers.
(Taylor and Hegarty, 1985, p. 142–43)

Cognitive processes of Chinese-origin young people

Regrettably, a literature search did not reveal any British studies on the cognitive processes of Chinese children and young people akin to the ones just discussed. An extensive survey by Taylor (1987), on the educational and social development of Chinese students in Britain, cites only six studies (including Lai, 1975; Fong, 1981; Cheung, 1975; and Garvey and Jackson, 1975). Taylor concludes: 'The limited data suggests that the ability of pupils of Chinese origin in mathematics is relatively high compared with other subjects . . . Indeed complacency about performance is unwarranted since the absence of information demonstrates that there has been no attempt at a proper assessment of performance' (p. 212).

However, the corpus of literature on this topic in the US is quite extensive (see Vernon, 1982). According to Stevenson *et al.* (1985), the high level of academic success of Chinese and Japanese students is well-known, and it has been hypothesized that this could be due to their superior basic cognitive abilities over those of American children. To shed some light on these issues, the authors carried out a comprehensive study with children (n = 240; aged 6.8–10.9 years old) belonging to three ethnic groups: namely, Chinese in Taipei, Taiwan, Japanese in Sendai, Japan, and American whites from Minneapolis, USA. A battery of 10 cognitive tasks and school achievement tests in reading and mathematics were used which had high reliability co-efficients. The results of this carefully planned study are lengthy and complex. The researchers summarize the findings: 'Similarity was found among children of 3 cultures in level, variability, and structure of cognitive abilities. Chinese children surpassed Japanese and American children in reading scores; both Chinese and Japanese children obtained higher scores in mathematics than the American children' (p. 719). The researchers concluded by asserting that the high achievement of Chinese and Japanese children cannot be attributed to high cognitive abilities alone but also to their experiences at home and school. The conclusion of this research reinforces the findings of the research discussed in the previous section of this chapter in highlighting the importance of the quality of schooling in the development of basic cognitive abilities and scholastic achievement. To this we must now turn our attention.

Scholastic achievement and examination performance

Compared with the studies on cognitive processes, the literature on this topic is vast. There have been several reviews of the research over a period of some twenty years (see Tomlinson, 1980, 1983; Little, 1975). The latest survey of research was undertaken by Taylor and Hegarty (1985) for the Swann Committee, which was set up chiefly to inquire into the reasons for the underachievement of some ethnic minority groups in British schools. At this juncture, it is important to remind the reader that the vast majority of Asian and other ethnic minority students currently attending secondary schools were born in Britain, and consequently have fewer educational and linguistic handicaps than those experienced by their counterparts of the 1970s and 80s (see Verma and Ashworth, 1986; Verma *et al.*, 1994).

Early studies

The earlier studies between 1960 and 1970 with 'immigrant' South Asian secondary school students found that their performance was generally lower than that of their indigenous white peers on English and mathematics attainment tests (Taylor and Hegarty, 1985). However, most studies (Ashby *et al.*, 1970; Dickinson *et al.*, 1975; Ghuman, 1980a) found that 'long-term' attendance at British schools generally brought their achievement closer to that of their white counterparts. Tomlinson (1983) drew this conclusion from her review of the research extant:

Asian pupils have tended to score lower than their white peers on tests of ability and attainment. Most of the studies undertaken in the 1960s and 1970s show Asians performing less well than their white peers, but Asian performance is improving with length of stay and length of schooling in Britain . . . Hindu and Sikh pupils seem to score higher than Pakistani pupils . . . Evidence on sex difference is equivocal.
(Tomlinson, 1983, p. 390)

The studies carried out in the late 1970s and thereafter with Asian students, who were either born here, or had full primary education in the UK, began to show performance on a par with their white peers on tests of achievement and even showed, in some cases, better performance on maths tests (see Driver and Ballard, 1979).

Examination results

Taylor and Hegarty (1985), in their survey of literature, cite over 30 studies and conclude that:

In spite of these methodological difficulties some tentative conclusions can be drawn. It certainly can be stated that Asians

do not in general perform worse at public examinations than indigenous peers from the same schools and neighbourhoods.
(p. 308)

However, the authors also draw our attention to the fact that, although South Asians' performance is as good as their white peers in inner-city schools (which both groups attend), it does fall short of the national norms. The Swann report (DES,1985) puts it pithily:

In general terms the findings of the two exercises, taken together, show Asian leavers to be achieving very much on a par with, and in some cases marginally better than, their school fellows from all other groups in the same LEAs in terms of various measures used.
(p. 64)

These measures included passes at GCE A-level (at the age of 18) and GCSE O-level and CSE (at the age of 16). More recent evidence on this topic, carried out by Smith and Tomlinson (1989), tells a similar story. They found the performance of South Asian-origin secondary school students in the public examination at 16 (GCSE) to be similar to that of the white students although, at the point of entry into secondary school, Asians scored below the whites. The researchers emphasize the importance of the quality of schooling and students' motivation in this 'catching-up' process.

A recently published research report (Gillborn and Gipps, 1996) on the achievement of ethnic minority students in England and Wales is of great interest because of its scope. It compares the performance of South Asians, mixed-race (for example, Pakistani/ white), African-Caribbean, Black and white secondary school students at Key Stage 1 of the National Curriculum (age 11) and at the end of compulsory school education (age 16). Regrettably, pupils of Chinese origin were omitted from the survey. The possible explanation for this exclusion is twofold: they tend to perform better than other ethnic groups, and their numbers are too few to make viable statistical comparisons. At Key Stage 1, the achievement of 2, 500 children from 17 LEAs (Local Education Authorities) was considered on the Standard Assessment Tasks (SAT). It was found that the performance of Pakistani-origin children tended to be lower in English, maths and science tests than that of the Indian, African-Caribbean and white children. The determining factor in the achievement of South Asians was whether or not the pupils spoke English at home.

GCSE results

For the purpose of this book, it is important that we now look closely at performance in the school-leaving examination (GCSE) at age 16. From a nationally derived sample, Drew and Gray (1990) analysed the results of 256 South Asians, 88 African-Caribbeans and 5,335 whites. The analysis took due account of the social class and gender of the students. The authors concluded:

For each one, there is a similar pattern. Young people from white backgrounds reported the highest results; the gap between them and the Asian group was mostly rather small. On the other hand, the gap between these two groups and the African-Caribbean group was rather large.
(p. 112)

No differences were found between the South Asian boys and girls but girls performed better than boys in the white sample. The study claims to support the findings of previous large-scale research in the field (DES, 1985; Kysel, 1988). Drew and Gray (1990) made no distinction between the students of Indian, Pakistani and Bangladeshi backgrounds. Gillborn and Gipps (1996), however, have presented an analysis which takes this distinction into consideration. They have analysed the GCSE exam results (1992–94) of ethnic and white students from various LEAs (Local Education Authorities) including Birmingham – the largest authority outside London. They conclude:

Indian pupils are achieving levels of success consistently in excess of their white counterparts in some (but not all) urban areas. Among South Asian pupils, those of Indian ethnic origin tend to achieve the highest average results ... it appears that in general, therefore, on average Pakistani pupils are not achieving as highly as their white peers.
(Gillborn and Gipps, 1996, p. 26)

Young people of Bangladeshi origin, in general, tend to perform below those of Pakistani and Indian origin. This is attributed to a number of factors, including high unemployment, a high proportion working in manual occupations and a less well-established position in the UK compared with other groups. Anwar (1998), in a recent review of literature, concludes:

From the evidence in the book [Anwar, 1998], we can conclude that Pakistanis and Bangladeshis are the most disadvantaged

groups, compared with Indians and also compared with whites.
Indians and African Asian young people are, comparatively,
achieving better in education, have greater participation in higher
education and, as a result, have higher qualifications than
Pakistani and Bangladeshi young people.
(Anwar, 1998, p. 190)

As regards the achievement of Chinese young people, there are no
viable statistics available for comparison but Gillborn and Gipps
(1996, p. 30) argue that:

Although they [Chinese] *make up more than five per cent of*
Britain's minority population, people of Chinese ethnic origin are
rarely concentrated in significant numbers in any single LEA.
Several of the returns we have examined indicate Chinese pupils
achieving significantly above LEA averages.

However, the authors caution us about placing too much confidence
in this conclusion as the numbers involved are small.

Post-compulsory education

The majority of the immigrants (despite their lack of education) were
from the middle strata of their respective 'home' countries and
entertained high aspirations for their children. Researchers have
found that people of Asian origin generally hold education in high
regard both for its 'potential wisdom' and its resultant occupational
mobility (Bhachu, 1985a, b; Fong, 1981). Consequently, they encourage
their children to stay on for post-compulsory education, and many
parents would like them to go to university for higher education
or/and professional training in order to compete at some advantage
with their white peers. The widespread racial discrimination (see
Jones, 1993) in British society gives a further impetus to this motivation
for higher qualification. The Swann Committee (DES, 1985) found
statistical evidence to support this contention, as did Craft and Craft
(1983). However, large scale research by Cheng and Heath (1993)
with controlled variables, such as social class, gender and parental
occupation, confirmed the earlier reports. Gillborn and Gipps (1996)
draw the conclusion that a majority of Asian youths are still in
full-time education (mostly studying A-levels) three years after the
end of their compulsory schooling. They quote from the research of
Drew *et al.* (1992, p. 64): 'Other things being equal, the odds of
Afro-Caribbeans staying on were three times higher than whites; for

Asians they were ten times higher than for whites'. As far as gender differences in staying on are concerned, more men tend to stay on than women. According to one source (Drew *et al.*, 1994), the participation rate of Chinese-origin 16- to 19-year-olds in full-time education is the highest (over 80 per cent) and that of Bangladeshis is the lowest (just over 50 per cent) within the Asian groups. Modood *et al.* (1997) found that twice as many Pakistani and Bangladeshi young men (aged 16- to 24-years-old) as whites were without qualifications, thus supporting the findings of other researchers in the field.

Higher education

The rates of admission of Asians to university and the former polytechnics have varied widely (Modood and Shiner, 1994). The authors present an analysis of the figures collected in 1992 from UCCA and PCAS – the then university and polytechnic admissions services in the UK, respectively. Whereas the Chinese have been hugely over-represented (twice as likely to be admitted compared with their percentage share in the 15- to 24-years-old age group at large), Bangladeshis have been slightly under-represented in both sectors. Pakistanis were over-represented in polytechnics but under-represented in university admissions. The Indians were slightly over-represented in university but did as well as the Chinese in the former polytechnics.

Modood's previous (1993) paper on the subject was based on the analysis of the admissions data for 1990 and 1991. The author summarizes his findings:

... In UCCA, not withstanding variations between institutions, the acceptance rates show a hierarchy with whites at the top, closely followed by the Chinese, with the Indians and Bangladeshis 5-10% below, Pakistanis about 15% ...
(Modood, 1993, p. 181)

The somewhat lower level of acceptance of South Asians is attributed by Modood (1993) to the fact that their A-level scores were below those of their white peers and this is compounded by the fact that they tend to apply for courses (medicine and accountancy) which require higher-level entry qualifications.

Vocational aspirations

The evidence presented in the preceding pages of this chapter would lead us to believe that Asian young people have high vocational aspirations. In the early 1960s, this was considered almost a 'joke' with teachers who were used to hearing from Asian parents: 'I want him to be a doctor or engineer . . .', and now accountants and pharmacists have been added to the list. These aspirations are grounded partly in the unfulfilled ambitions of parents, especially women, who were only able to find jobs on the lower rung of the employment market. Also, immigrants tend to have high motivation and drive to improve their social status in order to gain respect from both their own ethnic group and the host society. Verma and his co-workers (see Verma and Ashworth, 1986) carried out an extensive investigation in West Yorkshire, England, to throw light on achievement, vocational aspiration and related issues. A large sample of South Asian (n = 406, aged 16) and white (n = 656, aged 16) school leavers was tested to measure motivation and occupational aspirations; while a selected number (n = 200) were also interviewed on a range of social and educational topics. It was found that South Asian young people have higher vocational aspirations than do their white counterparts. The researchers argue that some teachers stereo-type South Asian children as 'over-aspiring', which is actually a misinterpretation of the facts since their educational achievement and positive attitude to school – which is incidentally higher than that of whites – closely corresponds to their high aspirations. A reply of one Pakistani boy is interesting:

My dad wouldn't want me to do what he does [dustman], *he would put me off that. Because he knows he hasn't had the education that I have or having at the moment and he would not been in that job if he had had some more education, so he knows I have got it and he wants me to make the best of it.*
(Verma and Ashworth, 1986, p. 102)

Eighty-five per cent of the South Asian parents took a great deal of interest in their offspring's future. Forty-one per cent of the Asian young people stayed on in school after the compulsory school leaving age of 16 compared with nine per cent of their white peers. The South Asian students had a more positive attitude towards school and education compared with their white peers. The researchers thought this may be due to Asian young people's perception of education as a means of social mobility. South Asian girls gave unemployment as the major reason for staying on for sixth form studies. Some Muslim girls, however, did not stay on at school or apply for particular types of job (for example, nursing, where they would be required to wear a skirt) because of the traditional outlook of their families. Of those who entered the job market, 38 per cent of South Asians were unemployed compared with 23 per cent of the whites. The researchers also found that some South Asian young people encountered racism from employers and this caused a lot of frustration and lowered their motivation. Consequently, Asians' self-esteem became lower than that of whites, whereas it was significantly higher when it was tested a year earlier while they were still at school. In both groups, the unemployed youth had lower self-esteem than those in employment. The career advice which they received at school was not only inadequate but the careers interview, in many cases, was devoted mainly to 'disabusing' [*authors' words*] Asian pupils of their unreasonable aspirations as noted previously in this section.

Teachers' attitudes to Asian students

For the successful adjustment and development of ethnic minority students (as indeed for all others), it is imperative that the teacher–student relationship is based on mutual trust and respect. Traditionally, Asians accord very high esteem to teachers. Teachers are considered to be mentors and guardians (gurus) of intellectual as well as of moral and spiritual development. The research literature (Tomlinson, 1984; Bhachu, 1985 a, b; Wong, 1992) demonstrates quite clearly the respect and trust which the Asian parents show to their children's teachers.

Discrimination and prejudice among teachers

However, it is a matter of concern that some teachers are not very sympathetic to the needs of Asian children and young people, and a few have been found to be racist. The Swann Report (DES, 1985) commissioned a research investigation into this topic. The team visited some 26 schools and, after intensive observations and in-depth interviews with a selected number of teachers, concluded that:

The whole gamut of racial misunderstandings and folk mythology was revealed, racial stereotypes were common and attitudes range from the unveiled hostility of a few, thorough the apathy of many and the condescension of others, to total acceptance and respect by a minority.
(DES, 1985, p. 236)

Verma and Ashworth (1986) conducted their research in West Yorkshire (as discussed at some length in the previous section) and concluded that they had found evidence of discrimination and prejudice on the part of a significant number of teachers. They quote verbatim from interview extracts to illustrate the pain and anxiety which the racism of teachers, often unintentional, causes to young people. Likewise, Basit (1997) concludes from her ethnographic research:

These stereotypical notions of the teachers have implications for the teachers and the ethnic minority children whom they teach. The teachers need to face their prejudices, not just racial prejudice, but class prejudice as well, particularly in the case of Muslim teachers.
(Basit, 1997, p. 109)

Ghuman (1995a) interviewed small groups of South Asian and white teachers on a range of professional issues. These included the perceptions of South Asian students in terms of their achievement and social adjustment at school. The white teachers in the research were of the opinion that South Asian parents do not give girls equal opportunities on a par with boys and that this is a cause of resentment amongst the former. A headmaster of a comprehensive school narrated the story of a very able Muslim girl to illustrate:

In one case the father would not let his daughter work within the area. So I paid her A-level correspondence course. She ran away from home to go to London to study law. The family caught up with her, as they always do – the network is amazingly good. They took her to her brother's house . . . The police said to the girl we can take you to a place of safety. But she replied: 'There is no point, they will catch up with me again. I shall never feel free; they will never give in.' They took her home and made almost a prisoner of her for three months and even now she is not free to contact us. She is not allowed to use the phone and to come to see us. Family blames us for interfering.
(Ghuman, 1995a, p. 49)

The other points made both by South Asian and white teachers were that South Asian parents do not attend parents' meetings and that some of them tend to have unrealistic aspirations which are not quite in keeping with their young people's ability. On the positive side, the teachers praised students' good behaviour, hard work and tenacity. They also showed some sympathy for the young people's predicament, especially that of girls, in having to reconcile the differing expectations of parents and school.

A comprehensive study (Smith and Tomlinson, 1989) of 20 multicultural comprehensive schools reported little racial prejudice as perceived by the parents. The authors noted:

Eight out of 2,074 parents interviewed mentioned racial prejudice among teachers. A much more significant proportion (4 per cent) said that the school did not take into account cultural differences or the special needs of ethnic minority groups'.
(p. 62)

Some researchers (Troyna and Hatcher, 1992; Gillborn, 1995) have criticized the findings of this study on the basis that the research methodology of the project is inappropriate in trying to discover the more subtle nature of teachers' racism and their ethnocentric attitudes; that is, the judgement of Asian culture and values by reference to their own norms. They suggest instead an ethnographic approach in studying such a topic as it requires painstaking observations of young peoples' behaviour and their interaction with teachers in a variety of situations, such as classroom, playground, library, school gym and the dining hall.

As regards the various policies and practices relating to multiculturalism/antiracism in British schools, there is a wide variation among the LEAs (see Taylor, 1992). There are some authorities which are pursuing and consolidating their aims and objectives on race-related issues but quite a number of the others have either diluted or totally given up on their initiatives.

Home and school

It is a truism to state that for the healthy intellectual and social development of young people it is desirable that there should be a good link between school and home. This cultural continuity between home and school may be achieved in a 'planned system' of schooling, where schools are set up to maintain the cultural and religious values of the home. In Britain, an example of this type is to be found in the denominational schools (for example, Roman Catholic, Anglican, Methodist), which were allowed within the state system under the 1944 Education Act.

One of the recommendations of the Swann report (DES, 1985) is that separate denominational schools for ethnic minorities should be discouraged in the interest of the wider pluralistic objective of education. Consequently, Asian parents are obliged to send their children to LEA-run multicultural schools. The ethos of such schools is naturally built up and sustained from British traditions and values and the vast majority of the teachers in these schools are white. Although there are many common objectives between the school and home (such as high academic achievement and good discipline), there is divergence of attitudes and values between the two on many social and religious matters. This divergence is chiefly in three areas:

- an emphasis on individuality as opposed to collectivity and interdependence;
- gender equality as opposed to bias towards boys; and
- a secular outlook as opposed to a religious orientation (see Ghuman, 1997; 1994).

The development of the first-named attributes is the major concern of the school whereas the latter are the preferred aims of the Asian home. Of course, it is well to remember that there is a wide variation even amongst Asians on these matters but, in general, Muslim parents tend to be more orthodox and traditional, whereas Hindus and Chinese tend to be more accommodating and flexible. However, the most contentious area for the South Asians is that of religion, because most parents would like to see some support for the spiritual dimension and practice of their religion in schools. But apart from the agreed syllabi on religious education (which tend to concentrate on comparative religions) and the morning assembly, the school ethos tends to be secular. Teachers encourage an inquiring and questioning attitude in their students which sometimes conflicts with the deeply cherished religious traditions of the South Asian family. Apart from religious matters, there is also a deeply-held tradition of respect for the views and opinions of elders which is being questioned by the younger generation. For instance, the views of the elders on arranged marriages is being opposed to the dismay of many parents.

In this context, it is interesting to note that a significant proportion of young people, especially of Indian and Chinese origin, is beginning to move towards the British custom of love marriages (Modood *et al.*, 1997). For these reasons, many Muslim parents believe in separate schools (religious and single-sex) within the state system where they can inculcate Islamic values in their children and young people (Modood *et al.*, 1997). However, according to one observer (Khanum, 1996), when it has come to voting on the issue, parents have tended to support the LEA-run school. Halstead (1994) sums up the dilemma of Muslim parents in Britain:

The problem for British Muslims . . . is that these two goals [maintenance of home culture and the benefits of modern scientific and technological culture] *cannot currently be achieved in the same educational institution. The second goal can only be achieved through attendance at a common* [state-maintained] *school, but such a school exposes Muslim children to what may be perceived as secular, non-Islamic cultural*

influences which the combined influence of the home and the
mosque may not always be sufficient to counteract.
(Halstead, 1994, p. 320, text in parentheses is added for
clarification)

The worries and anxieties of Muslim parents concerning their young
people have been well-documented by many academics (Anwar,
1994; Ashraf, 1988) as well as by Muslim organizations such as the
UK Action Committee on Islamic Affairs (UKACIA, 1993). However,
it must be stressed that the other religious groups in the South Asian
communities (Sikhs, Hindus, Buddhists) are far less apprehensive
of British schools. The middle classes are increasingly inclined to
send their children to private fee-paying schools in order to acquire
the many 'advantages' of accent, mannerism and confidence (*see*
Dosanjh and Ghuman, 1996) for their children so that they can
compete successfully with their white peers in the employment
market where they anticipate facing racial discrimination (*see* Cheng
and Heath, 1993).

Inter-ethnic relationships in schools

As noted by the Swann report (DES, 1985), schools are the only
places where ethnic minority young people are obliged to meet their
white counterparts amidst British traditions and ways of thinking.
Although many schools in the down-town areas of inner-cites have
become mono-cultural (that is, mostly Asian or black) or 'bi-ethnic'
rather than multicultural, even in these schools the majority of
teachers are white and the school curriculum is British in substance
and style. The Swann report envisaged the British school as fostering
certain aims:

It should also seek to develop in all pupils, both ethnic majority
and minority, a flexibility of mind and an ability to analyse
critically and rationally the nature of British society today within
a global context . . . The aim of education should be to ensure that
from their earliest years children learn to accept the normality
and justice of a variety of points of view without feeling
threatened . . .
(DES, 1985, p. 324)

The extent to which the aims and objectives of the Swann report
have been realized is difficult to evaluate as there has been little
research in this area. The situation is further complicated, however,

because of the change of policy by the Conservative Government in the period 1985–1989. During this time, and subsequently, the priorities of the Government shifted to 'raising standards' of achievement in all schools by introducing a compulsory National Curriculum and Assessment in England and Wales for all pupils aged 5- to 16-years-old, and there was a marked neglect and marginalization of multicultural and equal opportunity issues (Taylor, 1992).

Smith and Tomlinson (1989), in their large-scale study of 16 comprehensive schools, found that teenagers' choice of friend is overwhelmingly based on gender: 97 per cent of the boys chose a boy and 98 per cent of the girls chose a girl. As far as ethnicity is concerned, the researchers concluded that there is a 'fairly strong tendency' for individuals to choose friends from within their own ethnic group. But in the choice of friends, no particular ethnic group was popular or unpopular. Although the effect the ethnic mix of a school has on friendship could not be accurately assessed because of the small numbers of South Asians and other complicating variables, the authors concluded that it is likely that the policies and practices of schools have some bearing on the matter.

There is one substantial piece of research (Verma *et al.*, 1994) which focuses on inter-ethnic relationships, and a detailed discussion of its findings is relevant. The research method used is ethnographic: 'that is to say, it sought to yield its insights largely through recording the perceptions, opinions and conceptual categories of those who are in schools and who experience one facet or another of inter-ethnic relations' (p. viii). In addition, a questionnaire was given to a sample of students (aged 12- to 16-years-old) in nine schools in Greater Manchester and London, England. Overall, the researchers found 'the quality of inter-ethnic relationship to be quite good' in all schools, but more so in multicultural than in 'bi-ethnic' (Bangladeshi and English) schools. In one of the bi-ethnic schools, relationships between the Bangladeshi and the majority white young people were not good and largely reflected the poor and deteriorating communal tensions in the school neighbourhood. The best situation was to be found in a Church of England school which took students from some 80 primary schools and which reflected the very wide ethnic diversity of the London area and also the diverse socio-economic backgrounds of its pupils. The head of this school provided strong leadership and the staffing was quite stable. The school treated racist incidents seriously in that the staff were asked to report such incidents to a deputy head. The comments of children are quite illustrative:

We get on OK. I don't know why. Possibly it's because there are loads of different races in school.

And

They tell you if you're racist what happens to you. They tell in
assemblies and lessons. The school makes a big thing about it if
an incident happens.
(Verma *et al.*, 1994, p. 62)

As regards inter-ethnic 'mixing', the report found that in bi-ethnic
schools there was little mixing of the two groups but in multicultural
schools 'social mixing' was based more on gender than on ethnicity.
On the whole, teachers saw merits in inter-ethnic grouping in the
classroom but did not engineer it.

Racial abuse

The researchers found that the most commonly-reported incidents
in all schools were of verbal abuse related to colour or race. The
South Asian and other ethnic-minority young people mentioned
racist abuse more frequently than did the whites, and felt deeply
hurt because of the insult intended to them personally as well as
to their ethnic group. The students' ways of dealing with name-calling
were mixed but many chose to ignore it. All the schools had formal
documents relating to multicultural matters but only four schools
had explicit rules for dealing with racist incidents. As regards the
teachers' attitudes, the researchers note:

However, it was clear that a small proportion of students
interviewed (both black and white) felt that some teachers were
racially prejudiced in their treatment of ethnic minority students
in most schools; this perception was supported by one or more of
the teachers interviewed.
(Verma *et al.*, 1994, p. 102–3)

It seems from Verma's research that some teachers are still influenced
by their negative stereotypes of Asian pupils as noted by the Swann
Report (DES, 1985) over a decade ago, and this is a cause of concern
for those parents and others who believe in respect and tolerance
for all who live and work in multicultural Britain.

The research literature on Chinese young people is not that extensive
and recent studies are very few indeed. The latest survey by Taylor
(1987, p. 264) concludes:

. . . research suggests that many Chinese pupils suffer from a lack
of friends amongst other race peers and may be subject to racial
harassment of various degrees, much as their South Asian peers.
(p. 264)

Mother-tongue teaching and bilingualism in schools

Language is universally regarded as the core element of one's culture. It encapsulates our 'world views' and is the chief instrument for the transmission to posterity of values, attitudes, sentiments and skills. Some scholars (Baker, 1995; Cummins, 1988) argue that it plays an important part in the development of our personal identities and also serves as a social identity marker. For South Asian immigrants, their community languages (Punjabi, Urdu, Gujarati and Hindi) are important vehicles for the teaching of their religion. For the Chinese, the teaching and learning of their mother tongue is considered imperative for passing on familial values of filial piety and respect for, and communication with, elders. An experienced researcher of Chinese origin has argued:

> . . . the Chinese script requires a specific technique to form a word which by itself can convey its meaning in the form of a picture.
> . . . Therefore Chinese people usually regard the Chinese script as an intrinsic part of the Chinese culture. In order to identify oneself as Chinese, many Chinese people would insist that the person ought to know the Chinese language.
> (Wong, 1992, p. 50)

In the first half of this century, bilingualism was, by and large, considered to be a liability (see Baker, 1995) which, amongst other disadvantages, consumed a lot of the learner's time and effort and lowered his or her all-round mental functioning so resulting in poor performance on IQ tests. However, opinion began to change when systematic and controlled studies (Peel and Lambert, 1962) showed that not only do bilinguals score as well as their monolingual counterparts in IQ tests, but their bilingualism offers several benefits in the field of cognitive functioning and personal and social development (Bellin, 1995). Bilinguals have performed better than monolinguals in the *Divergent Ability Test* (use of objects) and have access to two systems of constructing meanings and for self-expression.

Minority language teaching

The provisions for the teaching of minority languages in British schools have been very paltry indeed due to the half-hearted support of the LEAs and the Department of Education and Science (DES). Two influential DES reports (the Swann Report, 1985 and the Bullock Report, 1975) failed to see the importance of ethnic minority languages in the maintenance of distinctive cultural identity and did not recommend their inclusion in the formal curriculum of schools. However, in a survey of research literature on South Asian minority languages, Taylor and Hegarty (1985, p. 188) concluded:

Overall there is considerable consensus across the relatively few studies on language attitudes that the South Asian language speakers value both their first languages and English. Their mother tongues are seen to have considerable importance for communication at all levels, for cultural maintenance and for identity.

Although there are no exact statistics available on the number of Asian young people who were actually born in Britain, it is estimated that, with the exception of Bangladeshis, the vast majority (over 80 per cent; see Modood *et al.*, 1997 and Verma *et al.*, 1994) are the third or second generation offspring of immigrants. In most cases (over three quarters, see Smith and Tomlinson, 1989), the first language of young people who were born in the UK is English but they also speak their community language. Smith and Tomlinson (1989) report, in their survey of 20 secondary comprehensive schools, that 85 per cent of South Asian students were bilingual to some degree. Furthermore, they found that, in general, over a third of South Asians (71 and 49 per cent for Bangladeshis and Pakistanis, respectively) attended supplementary schools to learn their mother tongue.

Chinese language teaching

The situation of the Chinese in the UK has not been researched to the same extent as has that of the South Asians, but a recent Policy Studies Institute Survey (see Modood *et al.*, 1997, p. 312) found:

Among the Chinese too there was evidence of linguistic decline with just four in ten of the 16- to 34-year-olds using a Chinese language with family of their own age, and nearly a quarter of all respondents not able to speak a Chinese (or Vietnamese) language.

From these figures, it can be inferred that 60 per cent of the sample (n = 196) used English within the family and that 75 per cent were possibly bilingual. Figures for adolescents are likely to be higher for speakers of English and lower for those who speak Cantonese or Mandarin. Wong (1992) surveyed the opinions of 244 school pupils and found that 65 to 70 per cent of the students used both Chinese and English, whereas only 20 per cent used exclusively Chinese, when talking to their siblings. According to the researcher, very few of the second generation can hold a conversation solely in Chinese, which can be a source of some distress to most parents and grandparents who do not speak nor understand English. Chinese parents in Britain have expressed their deep concern over the lack of provision for the teaching of Chinese in mainstream schools. In order to preserve their cultural heritage and language, the Chinese, like their South Asian counterparts, have established supplementary classes for their children and young people (see Taylor, 1987; Wong, 1987).

Smith and Tomlinson (1989, p. 93) describe the predicament of minority languages:

Minority languages in Britain have long been regarded, along with their speakers, as being of low status. They seldom appear on the modern language curriculum for all pupils and are thereby implicitly devalued . . . One of the most important steps that schools can take towards a multicultural education policy is to develop the teaching of Asian languages and literatures within the framework of the National Curriculum.

Dual identities

There is no empirical research evidence to date which directly links the use of the mother tongue (community language) to the development of self-concept or self-esteem. However, it is argued by Ervin-Tripp (1954) that a situation of 'dual identities' may be found to appertain to the speakers of two languages. Northover (1988) explored identity-related issues amongst Gujarati girls using the *IDA*'s (*Identity Structure Analysis*) conceptual framework developed by Weinreich (1985). The sample consisted of Hindu Gujarati-speaking young people from Leicester and Birmingham, UK. Two groups were identified within the chosen sample: Anglo-orientated and Indo-orientated. The Anglo-orientated group had significantly different values on the construct *Housework for both men and women vs. housework for women only*. They were uncertain and inconsistent when they used Gujarati to respond to the construct *Housework to be shared by both sexes*, but quite positive when responding in English. The researcher draws the conclusion that the girls in the study revert to an ethnically-based view of sex roles when answering in Gujarati. The Indo-orientated girls showed higher identification with the Gujarati traditions when speaking or responding in Gujarati rather than in English, but there was no difference in their evaluation of

British people when using either Gujarati or English. In this case, according to the author, the 'language context' does not make any difference because they have a positive experience of using the English language in their daily lives.

The researcher concludes:

Moderation of values seems to take place in the context of language in the case of Asian British boys and girls but changes are not always consistent with their orientations to British or Indian values.

(Northover, 1988, p. 14)

Therefore, from this study, it appears that the evidence linking the use of the mother tongue to role evaluation (as part of personal identity) is somewhat tenuous, and further controlled studies are needed to resolve the relationship between the use of ethnic minority languages and ethnic identity development. But, from a survey of literature, it seems that for many young people their community languages fulfil a symbolic need rather than a functional one (see Modood *et al.*, 1994).

Asian girls and schools

As noted in *Chapter 2*, traditional gender roles were clearly defined within Asian families. Girls from early childhood were brought up in such a way that they would grow up to be obedient daughters and would uphold the *izzat* (honour) of the family. Their schooling and education were planned in such a way that they would make faithful and conforming wives. As mothers, they were to be completely devoted to the care of children and of the extended family. Such a prescriptive role is not dissimilar to the one expected of Western girls before the First World War.

In Britain, there have been drastic changes in gender roles since the mid-1970s (Morgan, 1991), and the opportunities offered to white girls are now on a par with those available to boys. The British education system has responded positively to this change and has made strenuous efforts to provide equality of opportunity for girls in the choice of school subjects and career aspirations. Female teachers are increasingly to be found in senior positions and are providing role models for girls, who are out-performing boys in scholastic attainment at most levels.

School leaving age

Some Asian communities perceive schools as a serious challenge, even a threat, to the future of their family and its traditions (Thomas

103

and Ghuman, 1980; Anwar, 1994). Boys in such families often receive preferential treatment in the choice of clothes, friends, freedom from doing household chores and generally enjoy more independence. Some orthodox parents still want their daughters to leave school after compulsory schooling ends at the age of sixteen, although an increasing number of parents are allowing girls to pursue courses at local universities and colleges.

Thomas and Ghuman (1980) were told repeatedly by Bhatra Sikh fathers: 'Our girls should be allowed to leave a year early, so that we can prepare them for marriage, e.g. train them in cooking, housekeeping, embroidery and sewing' (p. 73). In face-to-face interviews, most of the fathers in the study pleaded with us to help them on this matter. Later on, we learnt from their daughters' teachers that the girls were often absent for several weeks at a time during the last year of their schooling. When parents were questioned on the reasons for their absence, the typical reply, according to the teachers, was: 'They have gone to see relatives in Manchester' or 'Gone to India to attend a wedding'. However, the reader is cautioned that the fieldwork for this research was carried out some 19 years ago with the first generation and we are now concerned mostly with the second and possibly third generations. Nevertheless, traditional attitudes still survive in some religious groups. A Muslim girl tells her story:

First, when I started school – my secondary school that is – my dad, he was on to me, like, I couldn't go to some kind of school and that, and he goes, 'My daughter's going to work hard and she is going to achieve everything there is and go on to further education . . . and in the third year, my dad suddenly goes, 'Haven't you done enough? Shouldn't you leave school? Shouldn't you pack up?'
(Wade and Souter, 1992, p. 7)

Teachers can be caught in a dilemma of whether to reinforce traditional parental aims and expectations regarding girls' education, or to teach them the Western values of autonomy and personal choice. Compromise solutions are being worked out by schools where there are good home and school links and where the teachers have won the confidence of parents. A teacher explained:

Yes, girls have less freedom. The girls cope well in school and the majority accept that home is different. I took 9a to see King Lear. This father wouldn't let his daughter go, but I persuaded him. We are finding the parents approach us about their anxieties. When

we assure them they [girls] would be safe, then they are more
willing. But not on residential weekends; very few would be
willing.
(Ghuman, 1995a, p. 51)

Choice of subjects studied

Some South Asian parents, though willing for their daughters to
continue with their higher education, still restrict their choice of
subjects as well as their career aspirations. The favourite subjects
tend to be sciences and maths, which are deemed useful for entry
into the teaching and medical professions. But, increasingly, the third
generation girls are challenging their families. An Asian teacher
illustrated:

Very definitely, I can give you a number of friends who were with
me in the sixth form, who had better grades than me who are
now married with children. At the age of 18 their fathers said,
'No'. Young girls are becoming strong now — they want to have a
choice of career. They are saying: 'Stop us if you dare, this is the
last time you would speak to me.' I am not saying they are happy,
but 10 years ago, no.
(Ghuman, 1995a, p. 51)

A study by Thornley and Siann (1991) reports no significant differences between the career aspirations of South Asian and white girls
aged 14- to 15-years-old in Glasgow. Nearly half of the Asian girls
aspired to a professional career in medicine, science, computing or
journalism. The remainder wanted to go for jobs more traditionally
classified as women's work, such as teaching, nursing and secretarial
work. Asian girls were less inclined to aspire to a career of which
their parents disapproved compared with their white peers, the latter
often choosing a career in spite of parental disapproval. Some other
interesting observations are made by the researchers:

What makes it more difficult for the South Asian and black
woman is her marginalisation in general. Discussions of sexism
in employment are often limited to the wishes, needs and
aspirations of white women . . . The separate and different needs
of women from ethnic minority groups are not considered. Racism
in employment is seen as something which affects the careers of
black men only.
(Thornley and Siann, 1991, p. 246)

105

To conclude, the researchers argue that the South Asian family's notion of *izzat* (honour), and the assumption that they intend to enter arranged marriages, place constraints on South Asian women's choice of career and financial independence.

Participation rate in higher education

Judging from the latest nationwide survey (Modood *et al.*, 1997), the participation rate of South Asian young people aged 16- to 19-years-old in higher education tells an interesting story. The overall participation rate for females is lower than that for males but there are within-group differences. Eighty-one per cent of Indian men and 66 per cent of women are in full-time education, compared with 71 and 54 per cent of Pakistani and Bangladeshi men and women respectively. An important point to note, however, is that although the proportional rate of Pakistani and Bangladeshi women is lower than that of Indians, it is quite close to that of whites, which is 43 and 56 per cent respectively for males and females. As regards the qualifications gained by the 16- to 24-years-old men and women, the report concludes: 'Bangladeshi and Pakistani young women, especially the latter, were considerably less qualified than average, and four out of ten Pakistani and half of Bangladeshis had no qualifications' (p. 75). Anwar (1996) advocates that the first generation Pakistani women, who are mainly from rural backgrounds, need special attention and that some opportunities should be provided for them in adult education. In sum, it may be inferred that the present younger generation of females is catching up with their white counterparts in staying on for further education.

As far as the scholastic achievement of girls is concerned, in general they perform better than boys. The Birmingham LEA's GCSE results show that girls outperform boys in all ethnic groups, save Bangladeshi, with Indian and white girls scoring five per cent higher than boys (see Anwar, 1996).

Summary

A survey of literature on education and schooling suggests that, in general, young people of Asian origin are achieving school examination grades as good as their white peers. There are within-group differences, though: Chinese and Indian youths are achieving above the national norms whereas Pakistanis and Bangladeshis are below. Asians' rate of staying on for further and higher education is significantly higher than that of their white counterparts.

As regards the ethnic relationships in British schools, the emerging pattern is an optimistic one. The researchers have found generally 'good' relationships between different ethnic groups but have emphasized the crucial role of the school, especially the head and senior teachers, in promoting harmonious race relations. It seems to be the case that clear policies (mission statements) and action plans on racism and bullying go a long way in fostering tolerance. The Asian communities value the significant part played by their mother tongue in preserving the cultural heritage and religious orientation of their community. From the literature, it becomes clear that schools may win the support and co-operation of Asian parents if they could implement, even if only to a limited extent, some provisions for the teaching of community languages.

Asian girls, especially of the Muslim and Sikh faiths, are likely to face many other difficulties because of the ways in which gender expectations of the home differ from those of the school and wider British society. These expectations relate to the choice of subjects and broader vocational and professional aspirations at school and to the restrictions placed by parents on progress to further and higher education.

Further reading

Gibson, A. M. (1988). *Accommodation Without Assimilation: Sikh immigrants in an American High School*. Ithaca and London: Cornell University Press.
Excellent coverage of scholastic achievement in Chapters 6, 7 and 8 as it concerns ethnic minorities generally and Punjabi Sikhs in America in particular.

Smith, D. and Tomlinson, S. (1989). *The School Effect: A study of multiracial comprehensives*. London: Policy Studies Institute.
A very good coverage of attainment and inter-ethnic relationships in secondary schools in England.

Verma, G. K. with Ashworth, B. (1986). *Ethnicity and Educational Achievement in British Schools*. London: Macmillan.
Based on the fieldwork carried out in Yorkshire, UK, and gives a readable account of scholastic achievement and related issues.

Wong, Y-F. L. (1992). *Education of Chinese Children in Britain and the USA*. Clevedon: Multilingual Matters.
An all-round sound text on the achievement and social adjustment of Chinese children and youngsters in Britain and America.

6

Reflections and Implications

Adolescence

According to Goodnow and Collins (1990), many parents expect that adolescents will go through a period of storm and stress. Erikson and his school of thought (Erikson, 1968; Marcia, 1994) has attributed this turmoil to identity confusion. Sociologists and anthropologists, on the other hand, have underlined the social factors for this predicament. It is argued that the different role expectations demanded of young people can lead to inter-generational conflict which in turn often becomes a source of anxiety and confusion. The media's reporting of young people's involvement in drug-taking, promiscuous sex, and aggressive behaviour (for example, at football matches) reinforces the stereotyping of adolescents' lives as being full of turmoil.

Coleman and Hendry (1989) suggest that while adolescence has traditionally been viewed as a stressful period in human development, critical examination of current empirical research indicates that the majority of adolescents pass through this phase without any major difficulties. This is reinforced by Durkin's (1992) observation that only about 5–15 per cent of the adolescent population shows severe psychological disturbance. However, there is some evidence to substantiate the claim that the use of drugs and number of psycho-social disorders has increased since the 1950s. Smith and Rutter (1996) analysed the post-Second World War data on alcohol and drug use and other psycho-social disorders of young people in the UK and concluded that:

> . . . *after taking account of the problems and limitations* [of data collection and methodology], *it must still be concluded that*

there has been a real rise in psychosocial disorders of youth in the post-war period.
(Smith and Rutter, 1996, p. 781, parentheses added)

Although the issues discussed in this book relate mainly to the concerns of Asian young people in the UK, they should also be relevant in understanding the development of their counterparts in Western Europe, North America, Australia and elsewhere. The reader is reminded that empirical research on children and young people of South Asian (Indian sub-continent) ancestry in the UK is plentiful. In contrast, the literature on the 'British-Chinese' is meagre indeed. On some topics, such as ethnic identity and scholastic achievement, there is very little research on which to base our deliberations and comparisons with other groups.

Home–school conflict

Asian young people share with their white peers most of the problems and challenges of growing up in Western multicultural societies. However, over and above the normal pains and joys of adolescence, they face two inter-related problems as noted in *Chapters 1* and *2* of this book. To recap, ethnic minority young people in Western countries often receive conflicting messages from their families and wider society about what constitutes 'proper' behaviour, values and attitudes (see Rosenthal, 1987). Additionally, most of them have to learn to cope with the racial prejudices of white society, which they encounter from their childhood through adolescence into adulthood. On leaving school and higher education, ethnic minority youth often face further discrimination in the employment market (see Cheng and Heath, 1993; Modood *et al.*, 1997). Asian girls, in addition, have to learn to cope with their parents' orthodox and traditional views, which tend to favour boys in all walks of life.

To overcome these handicaps, Asian families tend to urge their children to set themselves very high standards in scholastic achievement and to encourage (and even goad) them to study for those professions where there is a shortage of available indigenous personnel. Ogbu (1995) has studied in detail the educational aspirations and achievement of ethnic minorities in the US and comes to a similar conclusion, except in the case of the indigenous black (African-American) population. The reason for the latter's alienation, according to Ogbu, lies in their ascribed 'low-caste' position in the social hierarchy. Bullivant's (1987) extensive research with ethnic minority students in Australia also reveals a similar picture.

Development of ethnic awareness

The development of racial/ethnic awareness in children and young people was discussed in *Chapter 4*. It was argued that children as young as three years old (Katz, 1976) become aware of their ethnicity and soon after begin to attach feelings of 'likes' and 'dislikes' to their own group and to other groups. The research findings of both Milner (1983) and Davey (1983), with British-born South Asian, black and white children, have clearly demonstrated the 'in-group' preferences of children irrespective of their ethnic origin.

The *Social Identity Theory* of Tajfel and his co-workers (1978) has shed light on the importance of group membership in inter-ethnic relationships. Tajfel (1992) argues that the dominant group likes to keep its advantageous position *vis-à-vis* minority groups in all manner of things. The prejudice against Asian and other ethnic groups in the UK and in other European countries may thus be explained in terms of in-group versus out-group dynamics, which are often reinforced by the structural and institutional arrangement of society.

Stereotypes

The formation and significance of stereotypes in simplifying our social world was discussed in *Chapter 3*. Tajfel (1990, p. 441) defines it succinctly: 'Stereotyping can be considered as an inescapable adjunct to the human activity of categorisation. As such, it is neither "bad" nor "good"'. It was noted that negative stereotypes of Asian people are used by some white young people in schools. One of the tasks facing teachers, counsellors and school psychologists is to deal with students' negative racial stereotypes by engaging them on the media presentation of race-related issues.

Social adaptation

In *Chapter 2* of this book the response to social adaptation of the first generation of Asian immigrants was described as being one of 'separation' – a minimum accommodation to the British way of life. In contrast, the research literature suggests that the second and new generations of young people are seeking 'integration'. Integration strategy in this instance consists of preserving core elements of one's ethnic culture, and combining and synthesizing it with key elements of British culture such as autonomy and gender equality. In practical terms what this integration means for Asian youths may include: some form of bilingualism; taking heed of religious teachings and upholding the family *izzat* (honour and values); and some freedom to choose careers, friends and marriage partners. There are other less controversial areas of bi-culturalism, namely: leisure-time pursuits, mixed food, *Bhangra* music, and clothes fashion, which most South Asian young people are pursuing with great zeal (Ghuman, 1994; Drury, 1991). Modood *et al.* (1997) report that nearly half of their sample of South Asian young people thought themselves to be 'culturally' British while still retaining a feeling of 'belonging' to their own religious communities. Young people of Asian ancestry also prefer a similar strategy in the USA, according to Helweg and Helweg (1990). Likewise Sam's (1994) studies of younger generations (of immigrant ancestry) in Norway found that:

Even though these children originated from traditional societies and cultures that are different from that of their present host society, the present study suggests that the children are reluctant to give up these traditional cultural norms and values and replace them with that of the mainstream society . . . integration comes out to be the most common mode of acculturation.
(1992, p. 15)

Phinney (1996) argues that it is important for both white and non-white youths to explore their ethnicities. For the former, it should lead to better understanding of existing (white) racism and the privileged position of their own ethnic group and, for the latter, it should help to develop an understanding and acceptance of their cultural traditions and the contribution they have made to wider society. Likewise, Hutnik (1991) suggests that acculturation policies in Britain would provide minority groups with not only functional knowledge of the British way of life but would enable them to explore their own ethnicity. A study by de Domanico *et al.* (1994) with Mexican American adolescents found that '. . . bicultural adolescents may be better adjusted, more flexible, and better able to mediate acculturative stress in culturally ambiguous circumstances' (p. 197). Berry (1997) also advocates integration as a more humane and functional strategy for Canada and for other multicultural societies to adopt and implement.

Relationships

Marriages across ethnic/racial divides are likely to increase with subsequent generations (see Modood *et al.*, 1997). Children of mixed marriages may have a distinctive problem of self-identification. As discussed in *Chapter 3* of this book, the research on 'mixed' (black and white, see Tizard and Phoenix, 1993) young people has revealed a complex picture of their adaptation. It was found that most young people are proud of their mixed parentage – the majority (60 per cent) showing a positive racial identity. However, the researchers conclude:

It is still not an easy ride to be of mixed black and white parentage in our society – because of racism, the situation is very different from that of, say, children with one parent British and one French parent.

They also discovered factors of neighbourhood, geographical region, school attended, social class, family dynamics, all of which affect identity and adaptation. There is very little research on this subject with mixed Asian/white people. This neglected but important area needs exploration in view of the increasing number of 'mixed-marriages' in the UK and elsewhere.

Issues of gender

Throughout this book, the discussion of gender-related issues has highlighted the predicament of Asian girls. Many of them are still encountering a dual handicap: the one imposed by their parents and the other (racism and exclusion) by the wider society. Despite these disadvantages, their scholastic achievement is as high, if not higher, than boys. Both South Asians (save Hindus) and Chinese parents are less keen to allow girls to progress to further and higher education. Girls are also restricted, mostly by parents and in some cases by teachers, in their choice of careers. As a consequence of these additional handicaps of social adjustment, some young girls seem to suffer from psychological tension and acute anxiety, which in turn has caused serious illnesses (see *Chapter 3*). Studies on the eating disorders of South Asian girls were reviewed in *Chapter 3* and it was concluded that there is cause for concern and that those of Muslim and Sikh faiths, especially, might need extra help in coping with the disadvantages imposed by their parents and the wider society. It is interesting to note, however, that according to some researchers (for example, Frydenberg, 1997; Groer *et al.*, 1992; Peterson, 1988), teenage girls, in general, report stressful events and being affected by stressful events more than do boys.

Employment issues

As noted in *Chapter 3*, the rate of unemployment of South Asian and black youths is nearly twice the rate of whites in some parts of the UK (Anwar, 1998; Jones, 1993; Brown, 1985). Long-term unemployment has bred cynicism and alienation in some youths. Consequently, to the shock of their parents, some youngsters are drifting into a life of petty crime, prostitution and drug-trafficking. In Berry's model, such a process of alienation is termed *marginalization* (also see Hutnik, 1991). It appears that some young people are prone to reject both their parents' culture and the British way of life, the former because it denies them personal freedom and choice, and the latter because they face racial discrimination in employment and harassment from the police. Parekh (1995) analysed the situation in the aftermath of rioting in Bradford, England:

Drug-taking has increased within the Asian community, and so has drug-related crime . . . All this has naturally worried the Muslim community. It undermines their traditional values, subverts their family life and heightens the inescapable inter-generational tensions within the Muslim community . . . As inner-city areas become cultural deserts and fall prey to commercial exploitation of drugs and sex, those condemned to live there feel beleaguered.
(Parekh, 1995, p. 15)

There have been running fights between gangs of Sikh and Muslim youths in Slough, near London, and in the British Midlands, despite the pleas for restraint from their elders. Most of the gang members seem to be disenchanted youths who are venting their anger on one another's community property. There have been other such gang fights in the North of England (*The Guardian*, 24 July, 1992). A social worker from Birmingham gave the present author (Ghuman, 1994, p. 134) an account of these events:

Asian communities are too busy with the old order of things . . . the Koran says this and that. These kids are facing different sorts of problems: threat of unemployment, rigid restrictions of family, particularly on girls, drugs and so on. I find it quite frustrating . . . I say cultures change, these kids are bicultural and living in England not in Pakistan and parents should wake up to this reality.

Implications for the caring professions

Schools and teachers

A detailed discussion of ethnic identity issues leads us to conclude that, although there is no conclusive evidence from British studies about its saliency to social functioning (see Hutnik, 1991), the research in the US (Phinney, 1992) and Australia (Rosenthal, 1987) has empirically established its significance. They found that ethnic minority young people, with the exception of only a few, regard the 'achievement' of their ethnic identity to be an important part of their ego-identity. One of the ways to facilitate this development, in my view, is to accord due recognition to ethnic minority languages.

Languages

The role of the mother tongue is deemed crucial in maintaining inter-generational links and in the teaching and learning of religion and its rituals. Most Asian parents care deeply for their community languages and would like them included in the school curriculum (Wong, 1987; Bhachu, 1985a, b). Despite the practical difficulties involved in the teaching of several different ethnic languages, schools may seriously consider (and many have done so) implementing a policy of multilingualism/bilingualism and teaching as many minority languages as possible. Apart from the many cognitive and affective benefits to the pupils (Baker, 1995), such a strategy should bring schools closer to the communities they serve. There is a further advantage to be gained if bilingualism is seen to be the norm of a school. The majority of white students may not only try their hand at ethnic minority languages, but show more enthusiasm towards the learning of European languages. This should not be at the cost of meeting the special needs of a significant number of Asian students who need to be taught English as a second language, their first language being a community language. In fact, what is advocated here is a bilingual education policy similar to the one implemented in Wales (*see* Jones and Ghuman, 1995), which has been eminently successful in producing students who are balanced bilinguals.

Counselling

One of the positive features of North American high schools is an elaborate system of student counselling. All students are assigned to a counsellor who looks after their academic and personal progress throughout their secondary schooling. The counsellors of ethnic minority students have usually followed a special course and many have experience of living and working in a multicultural context. The counsellors' knowledge of the cultural and religious backgrounds of ethnic minority young people is often extensive (Ghuman, 1994; Gibson, 1988). Schools in the UK have never shown any interest in employing student counsellors. Apart from the extra financial burden on the shrinking resources of schools, there is teachers' professional antipathy towards the counselling services. The best hope is that multicultural schools will consider employing (and some already do) home–school link teachers with relevant linguistic and cultural backgrounds. Such a policy could provide much needed pastoral care for those Asian young people who find it difficult to cope with their bi-culturalism.

The Arts

It is quite possible for teachers and others to exploit the psychological tension and anxiety caused by the 'culture conflict' syndrome for a creative purpose. As noted in the preface to this book, Meera Syal (1997), a writer of Punjabi origin, has written a novel and made a film (*Bhaji on the Beach*) which draws heavily from her own bicultural childhood experiences in the British Midlands. There are other writers of note (Hanif Kureishi – *The Buddha of Suburbia*; V.S. Naipaul – *Home Coming*; Salman Rushdie – *The Moor's Last Sigh*) who have capitalized on their inner turmoil of living in two distinctive cultural traditions. Likewise, intellectuals and writers of Jewish ancestry in Europe (for example, Berlin, Steiner, Kafka) have creatively utilized the ensuing conflict and impulses of living in a traditional religious-led home culture, on the one hand, amid the secular and individualistic ways of the West on the other.

Educational psychologists and social workers

Collectivism vs. individualism

Some of the work which is carried out by the counsellors in North America is the province of educational psychologists in Britain. Dwivedi and Varma (1996) have made some telling points concerning the role of educational psychologists. One of the crucial points to emerge from their analysis is that school psychologists, social workers and other professionals should pay heed to the 'collective and cohesive' nature of the Asian family when dealing with Asian children and adolescents. As the professional training of the caring professional emphasizes an individualistic approach to counselling, they usually find it hard to empathize with Asian parents' concerns about community connectedness and religious imperatives. Dwivedi puts it succinctly:

In western culture, relationships of the individual to society are viewed from an 'ego-centric' perspective, for example focusing on the reproduction of individuals rather than on the reproduction of relationships, with an emphasis on separateness, clear boundaries,

individuality and autonomy within the relationships, while in eastern cultures there is a 'sociocentric' conception of these relationships.
(Dwivedi, 1996, p. 22)

It may be argued that the impetus for change from the collective orientation towards individual orientation should be placed squarely on the shoulders of immigrants themselves, who have voluntarily chosen to settle in the UK, and not on the professionals. The force of this argument cannot be denied, but it is relevant to point out that many immigrant parents are changing, and others have already done so (Stopes-Roe and Cochrane, 1990). For instance, only a small proportion of second generation Sikh men wear turbans (under a third of the proportion of the first generation – see Modood *et al.*, 1994) and many have omitted their middle-names, in order to anglicize their names as discussed in *Chapter 3*.

However, the fact remains that most Asian immigrants belonged to very traditional rural backgrounds and have had to cope with two radical changes in their lives: the first of adapting to large urban cities; and the second of major culture change, for which they need help and support from the caring professionals. It may also be argued that western societies lay undue emphasis on individualism and this may not always prove to be a virtue. A 'middle path' (the *Madhym Marg* of the Buddhist) of inter-dependence might prove to be a better perspective both for the individual and society.

Dwivedi and Varma (1996) present many case studies to illustrate some of the problems which South Asian parents and their young people encounter with educational psychologists and social workers in the UK:

Soraya, a 16-year-old Pakistani Muslim girl, was taken into care after her uncle and father had beaten her for attempting to go out with an Indian Hindu boy of whom they disapproved. The white professionals involved strongly disapproved of the father's views and had made little effort to mediate between the various relatives who might have allowed for some rapprochement to be found between Soraya and her father without either having to harden their position . . . Soraya made secret arrangements to marry the boy, despite the indications that neither of them was ready for the marriage.
(Maitra and Miller, 1996, p. 111)

The involvement of other family members when dealing with Asian young people is desirable as has been argued by many Asian educational psychologists (*see* Kumar, 1988).

Anti-racist policies

A working group of educational psychologists in England and Wales produced a report (Wolfendale *et al.*, 1988) on the training and practice of their professionals in a multicultural British society. The report indicates that educational psychologists are beginning to realize the need to develop anti-racist policies in order to promote equal opportunity. However, a survey of courses offered to educational psychologists in England and Wales concluded that courses in general did not seem to be adequately addressing multicultural issues. Since publication of this report, the senior editor of the report (Wolfendale, 1997– personal communication) has informed the present author that all the courses in England and Wales have subsequently formulated an equal opportunity policy, and the survey of 1987 (with some additional questions) will be repeated in order to assess accurately what has been accomplished in the interim.

Coping strategies

There has been a growing interest in the coping strategies of young people in modern times (Lazarus, 1991; Frydenberg, 1997). Coping strategies, according to Frydenberg, vary from individual to individual and are highly context-dependent. Temperamental traits and the family origin of an individual are important factors, as is the adolescent's past history of success or failure in formulating coping strategies. On cultural differences in coping, Frydenberg (1997, p. 203) writes:

However, where there is a cultural or ethnic mix, as in some communities, the differences between groups can provide a backdrop for informed discourse about coping differences ... The cultural determinants not only need to be taken into account but cross-cultural interchange about coping may improve young people's capacity to understand both their own actions and those of others.

It has been argued that professionals dealing with ethnic minority young people should be aware of the coping skills of their clients' parents, who had to learn the hard way how to cope with the prejudices of white society (Sattler, 1982). Analysis of current research on coping strategies reinforces the insights of those cross-cultural psychologists who consider social background factors to be imperative in the counselling and pastoral care work done with ethnic minority clients.

Conclusion

Modern theories of adolescence stress an interdisciplinary approach to understanding the pains, pleasure and problems of developing adolescents. Such theories (Coleman, 1978; Coleman and Hendry, 1989; Peterson, 1988) have attempted to combine and synthesize perspectives from both developmental and social psychology with the insights derived from sociology and anthropology. The evidence from a variety of sources suggests that there is a fair degree of support for the stance of Coleman and Hendry (1989), who propose a 'focal' model for such a venture. The writers argue that traditional theories have failed to adequately explain the fact that most adolescents – contrary to the predictions – do not in fact suffer from the expected 'storms and stress' of development. They explain this phenomenon by proposing that 'they cope by dealing with one issue at a time. They spread it over a span of years . . .'.

The authors claim two advantages for their model: that it is based on empirical research, and that it adequately explains the successful coping behaviour of most of the adolescent population. Empirical research from a variety of cultural contexts is cited in support of the model (Simmons and Blyth, 1987; Meadows, 1986; Kroger, 1985). In my view, the term 'model' is used too loosely ('perspective' may be more appropriate) by the authors to describe an approach to personal problem-solving which, after all, is robust common sense for most people. The fact that most young people learn to deal with their problems sequentially, rather than simultaneously, is very much a reflection of the way in which most *adults* cope with their day-to-day living. As far as its relevance to the understanding of the problems of ethnic minority adolescents in Western societies is concerned, it does explain to some degree how the majority of Asian young people in the UK successfully negotiate problems of adjustment as they enter adulthood (Anwar, 1998; 1994; Drury, 1991; Stopes-Roe and Cochrane, 1990). For instance, most Asian boys and girls in their teens tend to concentrate on their studies and helping at home rather than dating and going out like their white peers, thus avoiding confrontation with their parents. Their dating seems to be deferred until they go to college or university, and even then it is more clandestine than open. Likewise, deferred compromises on arranged marriages and choice of careers and employment are worked out (see Stopes-Roe and Cochrane, 1990). An Indian girl gave an interesting insight into how she dealt with her problems:

My father would not let me go away from home to a university in London. Then I suggested that I could stay with my uncle and travel daily to the university. He agreed . . . Then my parents

were concerned that I was getting too old (22-years-old) and they should arrange a match for me. I said: 'Definitely not from India'. To which they agreed. Then I said: 'Let me finish my diploma course'. After that I turned down several boys and chose the one I really liked; it was a sort of compromise . . . There was never any question of dating or going out with boys.
(Ghuman, 1997, p. 5)

A recent collection of papers, co-edited by Phinney and Goossens (1996) on adolescence considers ways in which the individual interacts in the processes of identity formation. The conceptual and empirical papers in the collection present the concept of context as 'that which weaves together' and shows ways in which the interaction between person and context may take place. Phinney and Goossens conclude:

In short, individuals develop not only in interpersonal and community contexts, but also in historical and cultural contexts that are likely to be even harder for psychologists to study . . . and that empirical findings validated in one era and culture may not apply in another.
(p. 494)

The conclusion drawn by Phinney and Goossens is a timely reminder to researchers to bear in mind that racial prejudice and discrimination is a telling and significant factor in the lives of ethnic minority adolescents.

In any society, socio-political and economic factors (along with regional, social class and neighbourhood variations) invariably play an important part in determining inter-ethnic relationships and adolescents' life chances and lifestyles (see Coffield *et al.*, 1986). For example, the predicament of young people of Algerian ancestry in France can only be fully understood and explained by taking into account the unique legacy of French colonialism in Algeria, the ensuing 'bloody' war of liberation, the current political situation (with the rise of the neo-Nazi party under the leadership of La Pen) and economic factors. The lifestyles and concerns of young people of Turkish origins in Germany can only be appreciated if due consideration is given to understanding their particular socio-historic situation, that is, their parents' status as guest-workers (*gast-arbeiter*), who were not granted basic civil rights and liberties, unlike those extended to Commonwealth citizens in the UK. Nonetheless, there are certain common features which are to be found amongst all ethnic minority young people (especially people of colour) across Western countries. These have been discussed in detail in this book and include: bilingualism, racial prejudice and discrimination, dual-identity formation, conflict of home and societal values in certain domains, lower scholastic achievement, and gender role differentiation. Young people have to resolve these issues within the existing and 'immediate' socio-political contexts of the region and neighbourhood within which they find themselves. This book has spelt out in some detail how young people of Asian ancestry in the UK are coping with their own predicaments and how this can be of value to professionals working with ethic minorities in other countries and cultural contexts.

Further reading

Bhopal, K. (1997). *Gender, 'Race' and Patriarchy: A Study of South Asian women*. Aldershot: Ashgate Publishing House.

Furnham, A. and Gunter, B. (1989). *The Anatomy of Adolescence: Young people's social attitudes in Britain*. London: Routledge.
An interesting account of young peoples' attitudes on a range of issues – including racial prejudice.

Hutnik, N. (1991). *Ethnic Minority Identity in Britain: A social psychological perspective*. Oxford: Clarendon Press.
This is an advanced text on both the theoretical and methodological issues and should be useful to the reader who wishes to go deeper into the subject.

Modood T., Beishon, S. and Virdee, S. (1994). *Changing Ethnic Identities*. London: Policy Studies Institute: London.
An ethnographic account of South Asian young people's views on identity, religion, language and other aspects of their home and English cultures.

Roberts, H. and Sachdev, D. (1996). *Young People's Social Attitudes: Having their say – the views of 12- to 19-year-olds*. Ilford: Barnardos.
An up-to-date description of the attitudes of young people. Chapter 3 is on racial prejudice.

Verma, G. K. with Ashworth, B. (1988). *Ethnicity and Educational Achievement in British Schools*. London: Macmillan.
A readable and sound text on a variety of issues and concerns of South Asian young people in Yorkshire, UK, in the 1980s.

References

Aboud, F. (1988). *Children and Prejudice.* London: Basil Blackwell.

Aboud, F. (1993). The developmental psychology of racial prejudice. *Transcultural Psychiatric Research Review*, 30, 229–242.

Adorno, T. W., Frenkel-Brunswick, E., Levinson, D. J. and Sanford, R. N. (1950). *The Authoritarian Personality.* New York: Harper and Row.

Ahmad, S., Waller, G. and Verduyn, C. (1994). Eating attitudes and body satisfaction among Asian and Caucasian adolescents. *Journal of* Adolescence, 17, 461–470.

Akhtar, S. (1993). *The Muslim Parents' Handbook.* New York: Ta-Ha Publishers.

Allport, G. (1954). *The Nature of Prejudice.* London: Addison-Wesley.

Anwar, M. (1978). *Between Two Cultures.* London: Commission for Racial Equality.

Anwar, M. (1979). *The Myth of Return: Pakistanis in Britain.* London: Heinemann.

Anwar, M. (1994). *Young Muslims in Britain: Attitudes, educational needs and policy implications.* Leicester: The Islamic Foundation.

Anwar, M. (1996). *British Pakistanis: Demographic, social and economic position.* University of Warwick: Centre For Research In Ethnic Relations.

Anwar, M. (1998). *Between Cultures: Continuity and change in the lives of young Asians.* London: Routledge.

Anwar, M. and Ali, A. (1987).*Overseas Doctors: Experience and expectations.* London: Commission for Racial Equality.

Aries, E. and Moorehead, K. (1989). The importance of ethnicity in the development of Black adolescents. *Psychological Reports*, 65, 75–82.

Ashby, B., Morrison, A. and Butcher, H. J. (1970). The abilities and attainments of immigrant children. *Research in Education*, 4, 73–80.

Ashraf, A. S. (1988). A view of education – An Islamic perspective. In B. O'Keefe (Ed.), *Schools for Tomorrow.* London: Falmer Press.

Aurora, G. S. (1967). *The New Frontiersmen.* Bombay: Popular Prakashan.

Azuma, H. (1986). Why Study Child Development in Japan? In H. Stevenson, H. Azume and K. Hakuta (Eds), *Child Development and Education in Japan.* New York: W. H. Freeman and Company.

Bagley, C. and Verma, K. G. (1983). *Multicultural Childhood: Education, ethnicity and cognitive styles.* Aldershot: Gower.

Bagley, C., Mallick, K. and Verma, G. K. (1979). A study of Black and White teenagers in British schools. In G. K. Verma and C. Bagley (Eds), *Race, Education and Identity.* London: Macmillan.

Bagley, C., Verma, G. K., Mallick, K. and Young, L. (1975). *Personality, Self-Esteem and Prejudice.* London: Saxon House.

Baker, C. (1995). *Foundations of Bilingualism.* Clevedon: Multilingual Matters.

Baldwin, J. (1964). *Nobody Knows My Name.* London: Michael Joseph.

Ballard, R. (1994). Differentiation and Disjunction among Sikhs. In R. Ballard (Ed.) *Desh Pardesh: The South Asian presence.* London: Hurst & Company.

Basit, N.T. (1997). *Eastern Values; Western Milieu: Identities and aspirations of adolescent British Muslim girls.* Aldershot: Ashgate.

121

Baxter, S. (1986). *The Chinese and Vietnamese in Birmingham*. Birmingham: Birmingham City Council.

Bellin, W. (1995). Psychology and bilingualism. In B. Jones and P. A. S. Ghuman (Eds), *Bilingualism, Education and Identity*. Cardiff: University of Wales Press.

Bergen (Jr), J. T. and Han-Fu, M.I. (1995). An Analysis and Review of Confucian Philosophy as the Basis for Chinese Education. *International Education, 24,* 40–52.

Berlin, I. (1990). *The Crooked Timber of Humanity*. London: John Murray.

Berry, J.W. (1965). Temne and Eskimo Perceptual Skills. *International Journal of Psychology, 1:27,* 207–229.

Berry, J.W. (1976). *Human Ecology and Cognitive Style: Comparative studies in cultural and psychological adaptation*. New York: Sage.

Berry, J. W. (1992). Acculturation and adaptation in a new society. *International Migration, 30,* 69–85.

Berry, J. W. (1994). Acculturation and psychological adaptation: an overview. In A. Bouvy, R.R. Van de Vijver, P. Boski and P. Schmitz (Eds), *Journeys into Cross-cultural Psychology: Selected Papers from the Eleventh International Conference of the International Association for Cross-cultural Psychology*, 129–141. Liege: Swets and Zeitlinger.

Berry, J. W. (1997). Immigration, Acculturation, and Adaptation. *Applied Psychology: An International Review, 46,* 5–68.

Bhachu, P. (1985a). *Twice Immigrants: East African Settlers in Britain*. London: Tavistock.

Bhachu, P. (1985b). Multilingual Education: Parental views. *New Community, XII,* 9–21.

Bhadrinath, B. R. (1990). Anorexia nervosa in adolescents of Asian extraction. *British Journal of Psychiatry, 156,* 565–568.

Bhate, S. and Bhate, S. (1996). Psychiatric Needs of Ethnic Minority Children. In N. K. Dwivedi and P. V. Varma (Eds), *Meeting the Needs of Ethnic Minority Children: A Handbook for professionals*. London: Jessica Kingsley Publishers.

Bhopal, K. (1997). *Gender, 'Race' and Patriarchy: A study of South Asian women*. Aldershot: Ashgate Publishing House.

Billig, M. and Tajfel, H. (1973). Social categorisation and similarity in intergroup behaviour. *European Journal of Social Psychology, 3,* 37–52.

Biswas, S. (1990). Ethnic differences in self-poisoning: a comparative study between an Asian and white adolescent group. *Journal of Adolescence, 13,* 189–193.

Blair, M., Holland, J. with Sheldon, S. (1995). *Identity and Diversity: Gender and the experience of education*. Clevedon: Multilingual Matters in association with the Open University.

Bosma, A. H., Graafsma, T.L. G., Grotevant, H.D. and de Levita, D.J. (Eds) (1994). *Identity and Development: An interdisciplinary approach*. London: Sage Publications.

Brannen, J., Dodd, K., Oakley A., and Storey, P. (1994). *Young People, Health and Family Life*. Buckingham: Open University Press.

Breakwell, G. (1986). *Coping with Threatened Identities*. London: Methuen.

Broadfoot, B. (1986). *The Immigrant Years: From Europe and Britain to Canada*. Vancouver: Douglas & McIntyre.

Brown, C. (1985). *Black and White Britain: The third PSI survey*. London: Bower.

Bruner, S.J. (1971). *The Relevance of Education*. London: Allen and Unwin.

Bruner, S.J. (1996). *The Culture of Education*. London: Harvard University Press.

Bryant-Waugh, R. and Lask, B. (1991). Anorexia nervosa in a group of Asian children living in Britain. *British Journal of Psychiatry, 158,* 229–233.

Buchignani, N., Indra, M. D. and R. Srivastiva (1985). *Continuous Journey: A social history of South Asians in Canada*. Toronto: McMelland Stewart in association with Multiculturalism Directorate.

Bullivant, M. B. (1987). *The Ethnic Encounter in the Secondary School*. London: Falmer Press.

Burgin, T. and Edison, P. (1967). *Spring Grove: The education of immigrant children*. London: Oxford University Press for Institute of Race Relations.

Burroughs , G. E. R. (1971). *Design and Analysis in Educational Research*. Educational Monograph. Birmingham: University of Birmingham.

Chan, A. (1986). *Employment Prospect of Chinese Youth in Britain*. London: Commission for Racial Equality.

Chan, M. Y. (1994).The Chinese in Greater Manchester: A demographic profile. *New Community, XX,* 655–659.

Chan, M. Y. (1995). Chinese children and education in Britain. *Multicultural Teaching, 13,* 11–14.

Cheng, Y. and Heath, A. (1993). Ethnic and class destinations. *Oxford Review of Education, 19,* 151–165.

Cheung, W. C. H. (1975). The Chinese Way: A social study of the Hong Kong community in a Yorkshire city. Unpublished M. Phil. Thesis. York: University of York.

Child, L. I. (1970). *Italian or American? The Second Generation in Conflict*. New York: Russell & Russell.

Clark, K. (1955). *Prejudice and Your Child*. Boston: Beacon Press.

Clark, K. (1965). *Dark Ghetto*. London and New York: Gollancz.

Coffield, F., Borrill, C. and Marshall, S. (1986). *Growing Up at the Margins*. Milton Keynes: Open University Press.

Cohen, L. and Manion, L. (1983). *Multicultural Classrooms: Perspectives for teachers*. London: Croom Helm.

Cohen, R. (1991). East–West and European migration in a global context. *New Community, 18,* 9–26.

Cole, M., Gay, J., Glick, A. J. and Sharp, W. D. (1971). *The Cultural Context of Learning and Thinking: An exploration in experimental anthropology*. London: Methuen.

Coleman, C. J. (1978). Current contradictions in adolescent theory. *Journal of Youth and Adolescence, 7,* 1–11.

Coleman, C. J. and Hendry, L. (1989). *The Nature of Adolescence*. London: Routledge.

Commission for Racial Equality (CRE) (1987). *Learning in Terror*. London: Commission for Racial Equality.

Coopersmith, S. (1967). *The Antecedents of Self-Esteem*. San Francisco: Freeman.

Coopersmith, S. (1975). Self-Concept, Race and Education. In G.K. Verma and C. Bagley (Eds) *Race and Education Across Cultures*. London: Heinemann.

Craft, M. and Craft, A. (1983). The participation of ethnic minority pupils in further and higher education. *Educational Research, 25,* 10–19.

Cummins, J. (1988). From multicultural to anti-racist education: an analysis of programmes and policies in Ontario. In T. Skuttnabb-Kangas and J. Cummins (Eds), *Minority Education*. Clevedon: Multilingual Matters.

Daniel, W. W. (1968). *Racial Disadvantage in Britain*. Harmondsworth: Penguin Books.

Dasen, R.P. (1994). Adolescence in cross-cultural perspective. International Workshop on Education, Family, and Development in Africa. University of Abidjan, 5–8 April, 1994.

Davey, A. (1983). *Learning to be Prejudiced: Growing up in multi-ethnic Britain.* London: Edward Arnold.

de Domanico, B. Y., Crawford, I. and Dewolfe, S. A. (1994). Ethnic identity and self-concept in Mexican-American adolescents: Is bicultural identity related to stress or better adjustment? *Child and Youth Care Forum*, 23, 197–206.

Department of Education and Science (DES) (1975). *Language for Life (The Bullock Report)*. London: HMSO.

Department of Education And Science (DES) (1985). *Education For All (The Swann Report)*. London: HMSO.

Desai, R. (1963). *Indian Immigrants in Britain*. Oxford: Oxford University Press.

Dhaya, B. (1972). Pakistanis in England. *New Community*, 2, 25–33.

Dickinson, I., Hobbs, A., Leinberg, M.K. and Martin, P.J. (1975). *The Immigrant School Learner: A study of Pakistani pupils in Glasgow*. Windsor: NFER-NELSON.

Dolan, B.(1991). Cross-cultural aspects of anorexia and bulimia: A review. *International Journal of Eating Disorders*, 10, 67–78.

Donaldson, M. (1978). *Children's Minds*. London: Norton.

Dosanjh, J. S. and Ghuman, P.A. S. (1996). *Child-Rearing in Ethnic Minorities*. Clevedon: Multilingual Matters.

Dosanjh, J. S. and Ghuman, P.A.S. (1997a). Punjabi child-rearing in Britain: Development of identity, religion and bilingualism. *Childhood: A global journal of child research*, 4, 285–301.

Dosanjh, J. S. and Ghuman, P.A.S. (1997b). Asian parents and English education – 20 years on: A study of two generations. *Educational Studies*, 23, 459–71.

Drew, D. (1995). *Race, Education and Work: The statistics of inequality*. Aldershot: Avebury.

Drew, D. and Gray, J. (1990). The Fifth-year examination achievement of Black young people in England and Wales. *Educational Research*, 32, 107–117.

Drew, D. and Gray, J. (1991). The Black–White gap in examination results: a statistical critique of a decade's research. *New Community*, 17, 159–172.

Drew, D., Gray, J. and Sime, N. (1992). *Against the Odds: The education and labour market experiences of Black young people: England & Wales Youth Cohort Study*. Report R&D No. 68. Sheffield: Department of Employment.

Drew, D., Gray, J. and Sporton, D. (1994). Ethnic differences in the educational participation of 16–19 year olds. Unpublished paper presented to the OPCS/ESCR Census Analysis Group Conference held September, 1994. Leeds: University of Leeds.

Driver, G. and Ballard, R. (1979). Comparing performance in multi-racial schools – South Asian pupils at 16 plus. *New Community*, VII, 143–153.

Drury, B. (1991). Sikh girls and the maintenance of an ethnic culture. *New Community, XVII*, 387–400.

Duckitt, J. (1992). *The Social Psychology of Prejudice*. London: Praegar.

Durkin, K. (1992). *Developmental Social Psychology*. Oxford: Blackwell.

Dwivedi, N.K. (1996). Culture and Personality. In K.N. Dwivedi and V.P. Verma (1996), *Meeting the Needs of Ethnic Minority Children: A handbook for the professionals*. London and Bristol: Jessica Kingsley Publishers.

Dwivedi, N. K. and Varma, P. V. (Eds) (1996). *Meeting the Needs of Ethnic Minority Children: A handbook for professionals*. London: Jessica Kingsley Publishers.

Eldering, L. (1996). Acculturation Under Stress: Female-headed families in the Netherlands. Paper read at the 24th International Congress for Cross-cultural Psychology, Montreal, 15–22, August, 1997.

Erikson, E. H. (1968). *Identity: Youth and crisis*. London: Faber and Faber.

Ervin-Tripp, S. (1954). Identification and Bilingualism. In S. Ervin-Tripp (Ed.) (1973), *Language Acquisition and Communicative Choice*. Stanford: Stanford University Press.

Esmail, A. and Everington, S. (1993). Asian doctors. *British Medical Journal, 306*, 691

Esmail, A. and Everington, S. (1997). Asian doctors are still being discriminated against. *British Medical Journal, 314*, 1618.

Espiritu, L.Y. (1994). The intersection of race, ethnicity and class: The multiple identities of second generation Filipinos. *Identities, 1:2–3*, 249–273.

Eva, J. (1990). *Chinese Parents and Teenagers in Canada: Transitions and cultural conflicts*. Vancouver: British Columbia Council for the Family.

Fisher, D. and Echols, F. (1989). *Evaluation Report on the Vancouver School Board's Race Relations Policy*. Vancouver: Vancouver School Board.

Fong, L. K. W. (1981). Chinese Children in Liverpool. Unpublished Thesis, Diploma in Special Education. Liverpool: University of Liverpool.

Fong, R. and Wu, Y. D. (1996). Socialization Issues for Chinese-American Children and Families. *Social Work in Education, 18*, 77–83.

Fontana, D. (1988). *Psychology For Teachers*. Leicester: BPS Books (The British Psychological Society) in association with Macmillan.

Frydenberg, E. (1997). *Adolescent Coping*. London: Routledge.

Fryer, P. (1984). *Staying Power: The history of Black people in Britain*. London: Pluto Press.

Furnham, A. and Bochner, S. (1986). *Culture Shock: Psychological reactions to unfamiliar environments*. London: Methuen.

Furnham, A. and Gunter, B. (1989). *The Anatomy of Adolescence: Young people's social attitudes in Britain*. London: Routledge.

Furnham, A. and Stacey, B. (1991). *Young People's Understanding of Society*. London: Routledge.

Gaine, C. (1988). *No Problem Here: A practical approach to education and 'race' in white schools*. London: Hutchinson.

Garvey, A. and Jackson, B. (1975). *Chinese Children: Research and action project into the needs of Chinese children*. Cambridge: National Educational Research Development Trust.

Georgas, J., Berry, W.J., Shaw, A., Christakopoulou, S. and Mylonas, K. (1996). Acculturation of Greek family values. *Journal of Cross-cultural Psychology, 27*, 329–338.

Ghuman, P. A. S. (1975). *The Cultural Context of Thinking: A comparative study* of Punjabi and English boys. Slough: National Foundation for Educational Research.

Ghuman, P. A. S. (1978). Nature of intellectual development of Punjabi children. International Journal of Psychology, 13, 287–294.

Ghuman, P. A. S. (1980a). A comparative study of cognitive styles in three ethnic groups. International Review of Applied Psychology, 29, 75–87.

Ghuman, P. A. S. (1980b). Punjabi parents and English education. Educational Research, 22, 121–30.

Ghuman, P. A. S. (1986). Chinese parents' attitude to education and their children's achievement in Chinese. Unpublished paper. University of Wales, Aberystwyth: Faculty of Education.

Ghuman, P. A. S. (1991a). Best or worst of two worlds: A study of Asian adolescents. Educational Research, 33, 121–32.

Ghuman, P. A. S. (1991b). Have they passed the cricket test? A qualitative study of Asian adolescents. Journal of Multilingual and Multicultural Development, 12, 327–46.

Ghuman, P. A. S. (1994). Coping With Two Cultures: A study of British Asian and Indo-Canadian adolescents. Clevedon: Multilingual Matters.

Ghuman, P. A. S. (1995a). Asian Teachers in British Schools: A study of two generations. Clevedon: Multilingual Matters.

Ghuman, P. A. S. (1995b). Cognition and Culture: The nature of intellectual development of Indian adolescents. Scientia Paedagogica Experimentalis, XXXII, 275–290.

Ghuman, P. A. S. (1996). A study of identities of Asian origin primary school children. Early Child Development and Care, 132, 65–74.

Ghuman, P. A. S. (1997). Unpublished Paper. Aberystwyth: University of Wales.

Ghuman, P. A. S. and Wong, R. (1989). Chinese parents and English education. Educational Research, 31, 134–140.

Gibson, M. A. (1988). Accommodation without Assimilation. Ithaca and London: Cornell University Press.

Gillborn, D. (1995). Racism and Antiracism in Real Schools. Buckingham: The Open University.

Gillborn, D. and Gipps, C (1996). Recent Research on the Achievements of Ethnic Minority Pupils. London: HMSO.

Glover, G., Marks, F. and Nowers, M. (1989). Parasuicide in young Asian women. British Journal of Psychiatry, 154, 271–272.

Goodman, M.E. (1964). Race Awareness in Young Children. New York: Collier Books.

Goodnow, J.J. and Collins, W.A. (1990). Development According to Parents: The nature, sources and consequences of parents' ideas. Hillside, N.J.: Lawrence Erlbaum.

Goossens, L. and Phinney, S. J (1996), Identity, context, and development. Journal of Adolescence, 19, 491–496.

Groer, M. W., Thomas, S. P. and Shoffner, D.(1992). Adolescent stress and coping: a longitudinal study. Research in Nursing and Health, 15, 209–217.

Guennina, Z. (1995). Ethnic minority adolescents' identity in the New Europe: a transcultural approach. International Journal of Psychotherapy, 13, 52–59.

Halstead, M. (1994). Between two cultures: Muslim children in Western liberal society. Children and Society, 8, 312–326.

Handy, S., Chithiramohan, R. N., Ballard, C. G. and Silveria, W. (1991).

126

Ethnic differences in adolescent self-poisoning: a comparison of Asian and Caucasian groups. *Journal of Adolescence, 14*, 157–162.

Haw, F. K. (1994). Muslim girls' school – A conflict of interest? *Gender and Education, 6*, 63–75.

Helweg, W. A. (1986). *Sikhs in England*. Delhi: Oxford University Press

Helweg, W. A. and Helweg, M. U. (1990). *An Immigrant Success Story: East Indians in America*. London: Hurst and Company.

Hogg, A. M., Abrams, D. and Patel, Y. (1987). Ethnic identity, self-esteem and occupational aspirations of Indian and Anglo-Saxon British adolescents. *Genetic, Social and General Psychology Monographs, 133*, 487–508.

Horenczyk, G. (1997). Immigrants' perceptions of host attitudes and their reconstruction of cultural groups. *Applied Psychology: An International Review, 46*, 35–38.

Hsu, F. (1981). *Americans and Chinese: Passages to differences, 3rd edn.* Honolulu: University of Hawaii Press.

Hutnik, N. (1985). Aspects of identity in a multi-ethnic society. *New Community, 12*, 298–309.

Hutnik, N. (1991). *Ethnic Minority Identity in Britain: A social psychological perspective*. Oxford: Clarendon Press.

Jackson, R. and Nesbitt, E. (1993). *Hindu Children in Britain*. Stoke-on-Trent: Trentham Books.

Jones, B.M. and Ghuman, P.A.S. (1995). *Bilingualism, Education and Identity*. Cardiff: University of Wales Press.

Jones, J. M. (1997). *Prejudice and Racism*. New York: McGraw Hill Co.

Jones, T. (1993). *Britain's Ethnic Minorities*. London: Policy Studies Institute.

Kagitcibasi, C. (1997). Whither multiculturalism? *Applied Psychology: An International Review, 46*, 44–49.

Kakar, S. (1982). Setting the Stage: The traditional Hindu view and the psychology of Erickson. In S. Kakar (Ed.) *Identity and Adulthood*. New Delhi: Oxford University Press.

Kakar, S. (1991). *The Analyst and the Mystic: Psychoanalytic Reflections on Religion and Mysticism*. New Delhi: Viking.

Kakar, S. (1994). *The Inner World: A psycho-unalytical study of childhood and society in India*. Delhi: Oxford University Press.

Katz, P. A. (1976). *Towards the Elimination of Racism*. New York: Pergamon.

Kelly, D. J. and Weinreich, P. (1986). Situated identities, conflict in identification and own group preference in racial and ethnic identifications: Young Muslim women in Birmingham, UK. Paper presented at International Association for Cross-cultural Psychology, Istanbul, Turkey, 1986.

Kelly, E. (1990). Use and Abuse of Racial Language in Secondary Schools. In P. D. Pumfrey and G. K. Verma (Eds), *Race Relations and Urban Education*. London: Falmer Press.

Kelly, E. and Cohen, T. (1988). *Racism in Schools: New research evidence*. Stoke-on-Trent: Trentham Books.

Khanum, S. (1996). Education and the Muslim Girl. In M. Blair, J. Holland and S. Sheldon (Eds), *Identity and Diversity: Gender and the Experience of Education*. Clevedon: Multilingual Matters in association with The Open University.

Kim, U., Triandis, H.C., Kagitcibasi, C., Choi, S. and Yoon, G. (1994) *Individualism And Collectivism: Theory, methods and applications*. London: Sage Publications.

Kingsbury, S. (1994). The psychological and social characteristics of Asian adolescent overdose. *Journal of Adolescence, 17*, 131– 135.

Kluckholn, F. R. and Strodbeck, F. L. (1961). *Variations in Value Orientations.* Chicago: Row, Peterson.

Kohli, S. H. (1989). A comparison of smoking and drinking among Asian and White schoolchildren in Glasgow. *Public Health, 103*, 433–439.

Kondapi, C. (1949). *Indians Overseas, 1843–1949.* New Delhi: Indian Council of World Affairs.

Krishnan, A. and Berry, J. W. (1992). Acculturative stress and acculturation attitudes among Indian immigrants to the United States. *Psychology and Developing Societies, 4*, 187–212.

Kroger, J. (1985). Relationships during adolescence: a cross national comparison of New Zealand and United States teenagers. *Journal of Youth and Adolescence, 8*, 47–56.

Kroger, J. (1989). *Identity in Adolescence.* London: Routledge.

Kumar, S. (1988). A survey of assessment of ethnic minority pupils. *Educational and Child Psychology, 5*, 51–56.

Kysel, F. (1988). Ethnic background and examination results. *Educational Research, 3*, 83–89.

La Fromboise, T., Coleman, H. L. K. and Gerton, J. (1993). Psychological impact of biculturalism: Evidence and theory. *Psychological Bulletin, 114*, 395–41.

Lacy, J. H. and Dolan, B. M. (1988). Bulimia in British Blacks and Asians: A catchment area study. *British Journal of Psychiatry, 12*, 73–79.

Lai, L. (1975). Chinese families in London: A study into their social needs. Unpublished MA Thesis. London: Brunel University.

Lazarus, S. R. (1991). *Emotion and Adaptation.* New York: Oxford University Press.

Lazarus, S. R. (1997). Acculturation isn't everything. *Applied Psychology: An International Review, 46*, 39–43.

Leonard, K. (1993). Historical constructions of ethnicity: Research on Punjabi immigrants in California. *Journal of American Ethnic History, 12*, 3–25.

Leyens, J-P, Yzerbyt, V. and Schadron, G. (1994). *Stereotype and Social Cognition.* London: Sage Publications.

Likert, R. (1932). A technique for the measurement of attitudes. *Archives of Psychology, 140*.

Li-Repac, D. C. (1982). The impact of acculturation on the child-rearing attitudes and practices of Chinese-American families: consequences for the attachment process. Unpublished Ph. D. Thesis. Seattle, WA: University of Washington.

Little, A. (1975). The educational achievement of ethnic minority children in London schools. In G. K. Verma and C. Bagley (Eds), *Race and Education Across Cultures.* London: Heinemann.

Louch, R. A. (1966). *Explanation and Human Action.* Berkeley, CA: University of California Press.

Louden, D. M. (1978). Self-esteem and the locus of control: some findings on immigrant adolescents in Britain. *New Community, V1*, 218–234.

Maitra, B. and Miller, A. (1996). Children, Families and Therapists: Clinical Considerations and Ethnic Minority cultures. In N. K. Dwivedi. and P. V. Varma (Ed) (1996), *Meeting the Needs of Ethnic Minority Children: A handbook for professionals.* London: Jessica Kingsley Publishers.

Mann, B. (1992). *The New Scots: The story of Asians in Scotland*. Edinburgh: John Donald Publishers.

Marcia, E. J (1994). The Empirical Study of Ego Identity. In A. H. Bosma, T.L.G. Graafsma, Grotevant, H.D. and D.J. de Levita (Eds) (1994), *Identity and Development: An interdisciplinary approach*. London: Sage Publications.

Marcia, E. J., Waterman, A.S., Matteson, D.M., Archer, S.L. and Orlofsky, J. (1993). *Ego identity: A handbook for psychosocial research*. New York: Springer Verlag.

Mcguire, W. J., Mcguire, C. V., Child, P. and Fujioka, T. (1978). Salience of ethnicity in the spontaneous self-concept as function of one's ethnic distinctiveness in the social environment. *Journal of Personality and Social Psychology, 26*, 511–520.

Meadows, S. (1986). *Understanding Child Development*. London: Hutchinson.

Merrill, J. and Owens, J. (1986). Ethnic differences in self-poisoning: A comparison of Asian and white groups. *British Journal of Psychiatry, 148*, 708–712.

Milner, D. (1983). *Children and Race: Ten years on*. London: Ward Lock Educational.

Mirza, S. H. (1992). *Young, Female and Black*. London: Routledge.

Mistry, R. (1995). *A Fine Balance*. London: Faber.

Modood, T. (1993) The number of ethnic minority students in British Higher education: Some grounds for optimism. *Oxford Review of Education, 19*, 167–182.

Modood, T. and Shiner, M (1994). *Ethnic Minorities and Higher Education. Why are there differential rates of entry?* London: Policy Studies Institute.

Modood, T., Beishon, S., and Virdee, S. (1994). *Changing Ethnic Identities*. London: Policy Studies Institute.

Modood, T., Berthoud, R., Lakey, J., Nazroo, J., Smith, P., Virdee, S. and Beishon, S. (1997). *Ethnic Minorities in Britain: Diversity and Disadvantage*. London: Policy Studies Institute.

Moore, S. R. and Rosenthal, D. (1993). *Sexuality in Adolescence*. London: Routledge.

Morgan, O.K. (1991). *People's Peace*. Oxford: Oxford University Press.

Mumford, B. D., Whitehouse, M. A. and Plats, M (1991). Sociocultural correlates of eating disorders among Asian schoolgirls in Bradford. *British Journal of Psychiatry, 158*, 222–228.

Naipaul, V. S. (1987). *The Enigma of Arrival: A novel in five sections*. Harmondsworth: Viking.

Nehru, J. (1946). *The Discovery of India*. London: Deidan Books Ltd.

Nesbitt, E. (1998) (in Press). 'We are all equal': Young British Punjabis' and Gujaratis' Perceptions of Caste. *International Journal of Punjab Studies, 4:2*.

Ng, R. (1986). My People: the Chinese community in the North East. *Multicultural Teaching, 4*, 30–33.

Noller, P. and Callan, V. (1991). *The Adolescent in the Family*. London: Routledge.

Northover, M. (1988). Bilinguals or 'dual linguistic identities'? In J. W. Berry and R. C. Annis (Eds), *Ethnic Psychology: Research and practice with immigrants, refugees, native peoples, ethnic groups and sojourners*. Amsterdam: Swets & Zeitlinger.

Northover, M. (1992). Cultural identity and language: Young Punjabis in Northern Ireland. Unpublished paper. N. Ireland: University of Ulster.

Northover, M. (1996). Ethnic identity values of young Asian British people.

Paper presented at the XII International Congress for Cross-Cultural Psychology, Montreal, 12–16 August, 1996.

Ogbu, J. U. (1994). Understanding cultural diversity and learning. *Journal for Education of the Gifted*, 17, 355–383.

Ogbu, J.U. (1995). Cultural problems in minority education: Their interpretation and consequences. Part one: Theoretical background. *The Urban Review*, 27, 190–205.

Oppenheim, A. N. (1966). *Questionnaire Design and Attitude Measurement*. London: Heinemann.

Osler, A. (1989). *Speaking Out: Black girls in Britain*. London: Virago Press.

Owen, D. (1992). *National Ethnic Minority Data Archive: 1991 Census Statistical Paper No.1*. Warwick: Centre for Research in Ethnic Relations.

Pan, L. (1991). *Sons of the Yellow Emperor: The story of the overseas Chinese*. London: Secker & Warburg.

Parekh, B. (1986). Some reflections on the Hindu Diaspora. *New Community*, 20, 603–620.

Parekh, B. (1995). Bradford's Culture Clash. *The Observer*, 12 June, 1995.

Parker, D. (1986). Encounters across the counter: young Chinese people in Britain. *New Community*, 20, 621–634.

Parker, D. (1994). *The Chinese in Britain: Annotated Bibliography and Research Resources*. Bibliography in Ethnic Relations No. 12. Warwick: Centre for Research in Ethnic Relations, University of Warwick.

Parker, D. (1995). *Through Different Eyes: The cultural identities of young Chinese people in Britain*. Aldershot: Avebury.

Parker-Jenkins, M. (1995). *Children of Islam: A teacher's guide to meeting the needs of Muslim pupils*. Stoke-on-Trent: Trentham Books.

Peel, E. and Lambert, W. E. (1962). The relationship of bilingualism to intelligence. *Psychological Monographs*, 76, 1–23.

Peel, E. A. (1971). *The Nature of Adolescent Judgement*. London: Staples Press.

Peng, S. and Wright, D. (1994). Explanation of academic achievement of Asian-American students. *Journal of Educational Research*, 87, 346–352.

Peterson, C. A. (1988). Adolescent development. *Annual Review of Psychology*, 583–607.

Phinney, S. J. (1989). Stages of ethnic identity development in minority group adolescents. *Journal of Early Adolescence*, 9, 34–49.

Phinney, S. J. (1990). Ethnic identity in adolescents and adults: Review of research. *Psychological Bulletin*, 108, 499–514.

Phinney, S. J. (1992). The *Multigroup Ethnic Identity Measure*: A new scale for use with diverse groups. *Journal of Adolescence*, 7, 156–176.

Phinney, S. J. (1996a). Understanding ethnic diversity: The role of ethnic identity. *American Behavioural Scientist*, 40, 143–152.

Phinney, S. J. (1996b). When we talk about American ethnic groups, what do we mean? *American Psychologist*, 51, 918–927.

Phinney, S. J. and Alipuria, L. L. (1990). Ethnic identity in college students from four ethnic groups. *Journal of Adolescence*, 13, 171–184.

Phinney, J. S. and Alipuria, L. L. (1996). At the interface of cultures: Multiethnic/multicultural high school and college students. *The Journal of Social Psychology*, 136, 139–158.

Phinney, S. J. and Chavira, V. (1995). Parental ethnic socialization and adolescent coping with problems related to ethnicity. *Journal of Research on Adolescence*, 5, 31–53.

Phinney, S. J. and Goossens, L. (1996). Introduction: Identity development in context. *Journal of Adolescence, 19,* 401–403.

Phinney, S. J. and Rotheram, J M. (1987). *Children's Ethnic Socialization: Pluralism and development.* London: Sage Focus Edition.

Piaget, J. (1952). *The Child's Conception of Number.* London: Routledge & Kegan Paul.

Piaget, J. (1959). *The Language and Thought of the Child.* London: Routledge & Kegan Paul.

Pick, S. (1997). Berry in Legoland. *Applied Psychology: An International Review, 46,* 49–55.

Radke, M. and Trager, H. (1950). Children's perceptions of the social roles of Negroes and whites. *Journal of Psychology, 29,* 3–33.

Ranger, C. (1988). *Ethnic Minority School Teachers.* London: Commission For Racial Equality.

Rex, J. and Tomlinson, S. (1979). *Colonial Immigrants in a British City: A class analysis.* London: Routledge and Kegan Paul.

Roberts, E. R., Phinney, S. J., Romero, A and Chen, R.Y. (1997). Structure of Ethnic Identity. Under Review.

Roberts, H., and Sachdev, D. (Eds) (1996). *Young People's Social Attitudes: Having their say – the views of 12–19 year olds.* Essex: Barnardos.

Rose, E. J. B. and Deakin, N. (1969) *Colour and Citizenship: A report on British race relations.* Oxford: Oxford University Press.

Rosenthal, A. D. (1987). Ethnic identity development in adolescents. In S. J. Phinney and J. M. Rotherham (Eds), *Children's Ethnic Socialization: Pluralism and development.* London: Sage Publications.

Rosenthal, A.D. and Feldman, S.S. (1990). The acculturation of Chinese immigrants: perceived effects on family functioning of length of residence in two cultural contexts. *The Journal of Genetic Psychology, 151:4,* 495–514.

Saint, C. K. (1963). Adjustment problems of Punjabi-speaking children in Smethwick. Unpublished M Ed thesis. Birmingham: University of Birmingham.

Sam, L. D. (1994). The psychological adjustment of young immigrants in Norway. *Scandinavian Journal of Psychology, 35,* 240–253.

Sattler, J. M. (1982). *Assessment of Children's Intelligence and Special Abilities.* Boston, MA: Allyn & Bacon.

Sen, M. K. (1961). *Hinduism.* Harmondsworth: Penguin Books.

Sethi, R. R. (1990). Intercultural communication and adaptation among first generation Asian-Indian immigrants. Paper presented at the Korean Psychological Association International Conference on Individualism and Collectivism, Seoul, Korea, July 9-13, 1990.

Shaikh, S. and Kelly, A. (1989). To mix or not to mix: Pakistani girls in British schools. *Educational Research, 31,* 10–19.

Shams, M. and Williams, R. (1995). Differences in perceived parental care and protection and related psychological distress between British Asian and non-Asian adolescents. *Journal of Adolescence, 18,* 329–348

Sharma, U. (1971). *Rampal and His Family.* London: Collins.

Shaw, A. (1989). *A Pakistani Community in Britain.* London: Basil Blackwell.

Sherif, M. and Sherif, W.C. (1969). *Social Psychology.* London: Harper and Row.

Sikh Girl (1973). An Indian girl growing up in England. *Multiracial School,* 2, 1–6.

Simmons, R. and Blyth, D. A. (1987). *Moving Into Adolescence.* New York: Aldine de Gruyter.

Singh, G. and Passi, P. (1997). *Drug Use in the South Asian Community.* Blackpool: North West Lancashire Unit.

Singh, P. V. (1977). Some theoretical and methodological problems in the study of ethnic identity: A cross-cultural perspective. *Annals of the New York Academy of Sciences, 285,* 32–42.

Singh, R. (1988). *Asian and White Perceptions of the Teaching Profession.* Bradford: Bradford and Ilkley College.

Singh, S. (1966). *Philosophy of Sikhism.* Ludhiana: Chardi Kalan.

Sinha, D. (1996). Cross-cultural Psychology. In Pande, Sinha, D. and Bhawuk, (Eds), *Asian Contributions to Cross-Cultural Psychology.* New Delhi: Sage Publications.

Smart, N. (1968). *Religious Experience of Mankind.* Harmondsworth: Penguin Books

Smith, D. (1977). *Racial Disadvantage in Britain: The PEP Report.* Harmondsworth: Penguin Books.

Smith, D. and Tomlinson, S. (1989). *The School Effect: A Study of Multi-racial Comprehensives.* London: Policy Studies Institute.

Smith, J. D. and Rutter, M. (1996). Time Trends in Psychosocial Disorders of Youth. In M. Rutter and D. J. Smith (Eds) (1996), *Psychosocial Disorders in Young People: Times, Trends and Their Causes.* Chichester: John Wiley & Sons for the Academia Europea.

Steinbeg, L., Dornbusch, M. S. and Brown, B. B.(1992). Ethnic differences in adolescent achievement. *American Psychologist, 47,* 723–729.

Steiner, G. (1997). *Errata: A life of ideas.* London: Weidenfield & Nicolson.

Stephen, J. E., Fraser, E., Marcia, J. E. (1992). Moratorium-achievement (MAMA) cycles in lifespan identity development: Value orientations and reasoning system correlates. *Journal of Adolescence, 15,* 283–300.

Stevenson, H. W., Stigler, W.J., Lucker, G.W. and Lee S. (1985). Cognitive performance and academic achievement of Japanese, Chinese, and American children. *Child Development, 53,* 1164–1181.

Stonequist, E. V. (1937). *The Marginal Man.* New York: Scribners.

Stopes-Roe, M. and Cochrane, R. (1990). *Citizens of this Country: The Asian British.* Clevedon: Multilingual Matters.

Stopes-Roe, M. and Cochrane, R. (1992). The child-rearing values of Asians in Britain: A study of Hindu, Muslim and Sikh immigrants and their young children. *British Journal of Social Psychology, 29,* 149–160.

Streitmatter, L. J. (1988). Ethnicity as a mediating variable of early adolescent identity development. *Journal of Adolescence, 11,* 335–346.

Sung, L. B. (1967). *The Story of the Chinese in America.* New York: Collier Books.

Sung, L. B. (1985). Bicultural conflicts in Chinese immigrant children. *Journal of Comparative Family Studies, 16,* 255–269.

Syal, M. (1996). *Anita and Me.* London: Flamingo.

Tajfel, H. (1973). The Roots of Prejudice: Cognitive Aspects. In Watson, P. (Ed.), *Psychology and Race.* Harmondsworth: Penguin Education.

Tajfel, H. (Ed.) (1978). Differentiation Between Social Groups: Studies in the social psychology of intergroup relations. European Monographs in Social

Psychology) London: Academic Press. *Psychology and Race.* Harmondsworth: Penguin Education.

Tajfel, H. (1981). *Human Groups and Social Categories.* Cambridge: Cambridge University Press.

Tajfel, H.(Ed.) (1982). *Social Identity and Intergroup Relations.* Cambridge: Cambridge University Press.

Tajfel, H. (1990). Intergroup Behaviour: II Group Perspectives. In H. Tajfel and C. Fraser (Eds), *Introducing Social Psychology.* Harmondsworth: Penguin Books.

Tajfel, H. (1992). *The Social Psychology of Minorities.* London: The Minority Rights Group.

Tajfel, H., Jahoda, G., Nemeth, R., Rim, Y. and Johnson, N. (1972). Devaluation by children of their own national and ethnic group: Two case studies. *British Journal of Social and Clinical Psychology, 11,* 235–243.

Taylor, J. H. (1976). *The Half-way Generation.* Windsor: NFER.

Taylor, J. M. (1992). *Multicultural Anti-racist Education after ERA: Concerns, constraints and challenges.* Slough: National Foundation for Educational Research.

Taylor, J. M. and Hegarty, S. (1985). *The Best of Both Worlds. . .?* Windsor: NFER Nelson.

Taylor, M. (1987). *Chinese Pupils in Britain.* Windsor: NFER-Nelson.

Thomas, D. T. and Ghuman, P. A. S. (1980). *A Survey of Social and Religious Attitudes Among Sikhs In Cardiff.* Mimeograph. Cardiff: The Open University.

Thompson, M. (1974). The Second Generation – Punjabi or English? *New Community, 3,* 242–248.

Thornley, P. E. and Siann, G. (1991). The career aspirations of South Asian girls in Glasgow. *Gender and Education, 3,* 237–248.

Tizard, B. and Phoenix, A. (1993). *Black, White or Mixed Race?* London: Routledge.

Tomlinson, S. (1980). The educational performance of ethnic minority children. *New Community, VIII,* 213–234.

Tomlinson, S. (1983). The educational performance of Asian children. *New Community, X,* 381–392.

Tomlinson, S. (1984). *Home and School in Multicultural Britain.* London: Batsford.

Townsend, S. (1982). *The Secret Diary of Adrian Mole aged 13¾.* London: Macmillan Education.

Triandis, C. H. (1991). *Individualism and Collectivism.* Invited address to the IACCP Conference, Debrecan, Hungary 4 – 7 July, 1991.

Triandis, C. H. (1994). Theoretical and Methodological approaches to the Study of Collectivism and Individualism in U. Kim, H.C. Triandis, C. Kagitcibasi, S. Choi, S. and G. Yoon.(Eds), *Individualism And Collectivism: Theory, Method, and Applications.* London: Sage Publications Ltd.

Triandis, C. H. (1997). Where is culture in the acculturation model? *Applied Psychology: An International Review, 46,* 55–58.

Troyna, B. and Hatcher, R. (1992). *Racism in Children's Lives.* London: Routledge in Association with the National Children's Bureau.

UK Action Committee on Islamic Affairs (UKACIA) (1993). *Muslims and the Law in Multi-faith Britain.* London: UKACIA.

Vaidyanatthan, P. and Naidoo, J. (1989). *Asian Indians in Western Countries: Cultural identity and the arranged marriage.* Paper presented at the 2nd

Regional Conference of the International Congress for Cross-cultural Psychology, Amsterdam.

Verma, G. K and Ashworth, B. (1986). *Ethnicity and Educational Achievement in British Schools*. London: Macmillan.

Verma, G. K. and Bagley, C. (1988). *Cross-Cultural Studies of Personality, Attitudes and Cognition*. New York: St. Martin's Press.

Verma, G. K and Mallick, K. (1988). Self-Esteem and Educational Achievement in British Young South Asians. In G. K. Verma and P. Pumfrey (Eds), *Educational Attainments: Issues and outcomes in multicultural education*. London: Falmer Press.

Verma, G. K., Zec, P. and Skinner, G. (1994). *The Ethnic Crucible: Harmony and hostility in multi-ethnic schools*. London: Falmer Press.

Vernon, P. E. (1969). *Intelligence and Cultural Environment*. London: Methuen.

Vernon, P. E. (1982). *The Abilities and Achievement of Orientals in North America*. New York: Academic Press.

Visram, R. (1986). *Ayahs, Lascars and Princes*. London: Pluto Press.

Vyas, H. (1983). Education and Cognitive Styles: A case study of Gujarati children in Britain, Eastern United States of America and India. In C. Bagley and G. K. Verma (Eds), *Multicultural Childhood: Education, ethnicity and cognitive styles*. Aldershot: Gower.

Wade, B. and Souter, P. (1992). *Continue To Think: The British Asian girl*. Clevedon: Multilingual Matters.

Wagner, A. (1982). Ontogeny in the Study of Culture and Cognition. In A. Wagner and H. W. Roberts (Eds), *Cultural Perspectives on Child Development*. San Francisco: W.H. Freeman and Company.

Ward, C. (1997). Culture learning, acculturative stress, and psychopathology: Three perspectives in acculturation. *Applied Psychology: An International Review, 46*, 58–62.

Watson, L. J. (1975). *Emigration and the Chinese Lineage: The Mans in Hong Kong and London*. Berkeley, CA: University of California Press.

Watson, L. J. (1977). The Chinese: Hong Kong Villagers in the British Catering Trade. In J. L. Watson (Ed.), *Between Two Cultures: Migrants and minorities in Britain*. Oxford: Basil Blackwell.

Watson, L. J. (Ed.) (1977). *Between Two Cultures: Migrants and minorities in Britain*. Oxford: Basil Blackwell.

Waugh-Bryant, R. and Lask, B. (1991). Anorexia nervosa in a group of Asian children living in Britain. *British Journal of Psychiatry, 158*, 229–233.

Webster, R. (1995). *Why Freud Was Wrong: Sin, science and psychoanalysis*. London: Harper-Collins Publishers.

Weinreich, P. (1985). Rationality and irrationality in racial and ethnic relations: A meta-theoretical framework. *Ethnic and Racial Studies, 8*, 500–515.

Weinreich, P. (1989). Variations in the expression of ethnic identity. In K. Liebkind (Ed.) *New Identities in Europe*. London: Gower.

Weinreich, P. (1996). *Ethnic identity and enculturation/acculturation*. Paper presented at XII Congress of the International Association of Cross-cultural Psychology, Montreal, August 12-16, 1996.

Weinreich, P., Luke, L. C. and Bond, H. M. (1996). Ethnic stereotyping and identification in a multicultural context: 'Acculturation', self-esteem and identity diffusion in Hong Kong Chinese university students. *Psychology and Developing Societies, 8*, 107–69.

134

Williams, J. P. (1997). *Seeing a Colour-Blind Future: The paradox of race* (The 1997 Reith Lectures). London: Virago.

Wilson, A. (1978). *Finding a Voice: Asian women in Britain.* London: Virago.

Wilson, A. (1987). *Mixed Race Children: A study of identity.* London: Allen & Unwin.

Witkin, H.A. (1966). Cognitive styles and cross-cultural research. *International Journal of Psychology, 2,* 233–249.

Witkin, H. A. and Berry, J. M. (1975). Psychological differentiation in cross-cultural perspective. *Journal of Cross-Cultural Psychology, 6,* 4–87.

Witkin, H. A., Oltman, K. P., Raskin, E. and Karp, A. S. (1971). *A Manual for the Embedded Figures Tests.* Palo Alto, CA: Consulting Psychologists Press.

Wolfendale, S. (1997). Personal communication to the author.

Wolfendale, S., Lunt, I. and Carroll, T. (Eds) (1988). Educational psychologists working in multi-cultural communities: Training and practice. *Educational and Child Psychology, 5:2,* whole issue.

Wong, L. M. (1989). *Chinese-Liverpudlians.* Liverpool: Liver Press.

Wong, R. C. N. (1987). *Chinese parental perception of British education and children's attainment in Chinese.* M Ed. dissertation. Aberystwyth: The University of Wales.

Wong Y-F. L. (1992). *Education of Chinese Children in Britain and the USA.* Clevedon: Multilingual Matters.

Wright, C. (1992). Early education: Multiracial primary school classrooms. In D. Gill, B. Mayor and M. Blair (Eds), *Racism and Education: Structures and Strategies.* London: Sage Publications in association with the Open University.

Wylie, R. (1974). *The Self-Concept Vol. 1 and 2.* Lincoln and London: University of Nebraska Press.

Ying, Y.-W. (1995). Cultural orientation and psychological wellbeing in Chinese Americans. *American Journal of Community Psychology, 23,* 893–911.

Appendix: Aberystwyth Bi-culturalism Scale

Please answer these questions by putting an 'X' next to the statement that applies to you, or filling in the blank.

1. Sex: Male
        Female

2. I was born in Britain.

3. My age last birthday was   14
                               15
                               16
                               17

4. I went to primary school in Britain.
        Yes
        No

5. At home we speak only English.
    At home we speak only our Asian language.
    At home we speak both English and our Asian language.

6. What is your father's job?

7. What is your mother's job, if she has one outside the home?

8. Please state the religion of your family.

9. Do you take a community newspaper?
        Yes
        No

10. If yes, is this written in:
        Your home language
        English only
        Both languages

Below you will find a number of statements about Asians living in Britain. I would like to know YOUR OWN VIEWS on these topics. Please answer by circling ONE response for each question.
SA means STRONGLY AGREE, A means AGREE, U means UNSURE/ DON'T KNOW, D means DISAGREE, and SD means STRONGLY DISAGREE.

1. Girls and boys should be treated the same.   SA A U D SD

2. Schools should accept our traditional clothes.   SA A U D SD

3. We should attend our places of worship
   (e.g. Gurudwara, Mosque).   SA A U D SD

4. I have no wish to go back to live in the
   country my parents came from.   SA A U D SD

5. I would like to see boys and girls from our
   community going out with English boys
   and girls.   SA A U D SD

6. I would rather eat Asian food all the time.   SA A U D SD

7. We should always try to fulfil our parents'
   wishes.   SA A U D SD

8. We should celebrate Christmas as we celebrate
   our own religious festivals.   SA A U D SD

9. We are better off living with people from our
   own community.   SA A U D SD

10. Parents and children should live on their
    own and not with grandparents and uncles.   SA A U D SD

11. A woman's place is in the home (house).   SA A U D SD

12. Only Asian doctors can understand our
    illnesses.   SA A U D SD

13. We should learn something about Christianity.   SA A U D SD

14. We should learn to write our own language.   SA A U D SD

15. Sometimes we should cook English food in
    our own homes.   SA A U D SD

16. We should alter our names so that our
    teachers can say them easily.   SA A U D SD

17. I would only like to make friends with
    young people from our community.   SA A U D SD

18. Boys and girls should be allowed to meet
    each other in youth clubs.   SA A U D SD

19. I would prefer to live in an area where there
    are families from our own community.   SA A U D SD

20. We should visit the homes of our English friends.   SA A U D SD

21. Asian films are more entertaining than English language films.   SA A U D SD

22. We should ignore our own language if we want to get on in this country.   SA A U D SD

23. I feel very uneasy with the English.   SA A U D SD

24. There should be more marriages between our people and the English.   SA A U D SD

25. Men should make all the decisions about the affairs of the family.   SA A U D SD

26. I would not like our women to behave like English women.   SA A U D SD

27. We should be allowed to choose our own clothes.   SA A U D SD

28. We should visit English language cinemas and playhouses.   SA A U D SD

29. Marriage should be arranged by the family.   SA A U D SD

30. Our women should wear English (European style) clothes.   SA A U D SD

31. The interests of the family should come before the individual.   SA A U D SD

32. The quality of English life is better than that of Asian life.   SA A U D SD

Author Index

Compiled by Mary Kirkness

Subject Index

Compiled by Mary Kirkness